Been there, Do
Didn't get the T-Shirt

To Beryl
many thanks
for your support.
Paul,

by
Paul Duffin

Cover design by Claire Duffin

Other books from Paul Duffin

Not Too Bad (2016)

From the 1970's diaries of a teenage Brummie. Over £1800 raised for Guide Dogs.

"Enjoy this sparkling piece of modern-day local history made fun" (Review by JH)

And the Cricket Was Good Too (2017)

Fun and laughter following the England cricket team on 9 tours around the world. Over £1500 raised for Sense, the deafblind charity.

"Engaging and humorous, (from a non-cricket fan!)" (Review by JD)

Say the Leeds and You're Smiling (2018)

Proof that office life does not have to be boring. Over £1300 raised for Prostate Cancer.

"A very funny an entertaining read that everyone will enjoy"
(Review by BB)

When I were a lad in Brum (2019)

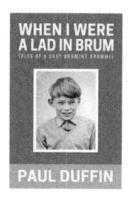

Fun and laughter all the way from age 4 to 17 in the blue-collar suburb of Yardley. Over £1000 raised for Alzheimer's UK.

"An absolute pleasure to relive memories of the 60's"
(Review by MH)

CONTENTS

Preface

Introduction

Appendices

PREFACE

As I launch this, my fifth book, I again realise the absolute pleasure I gain from writing. Being severely sight and hearing impaired has prevented me from enjoying so many pleasures such as music, theatre, television and mixing in groups. Thankfully my big AppleMac computer and a selection of magnifiers enable me to continue to write.

I thought long and hard before settling on a theme for book number five. A number of friends suggested that I should write a novel. I did consider the idea and have not dismissed it for good. I have put it on the too difficult pile for now.

Advice to new writers is always write about things you know about. My previous books have all had that in common. It occurred to me that lots of different things had influenced me with many of them not mentioned in the other books. Places, people and events came rushing back to me.

As I started to research my thoughts developed and the book has evolved to focus the things that have influenced me. Then adding anything of further interest found along the way. The first four books have helped Guide Dogs UK, Sense, Prostate Cancer UK and Alzheimer's UK. I know several people suffering from Parkinson's disease including a very good friend, Rob Sherratt. Therefore, all royalties from this book go to Parkinson's UK. My target is to raise £1000 which all the others have exceeded. Thank you for buying this and any of the others. Please help these great charities by spreading the word.

My very grateful thanks to my wife Sue who read every draft having been there herself for most of the events. Our daughter Claire has again used her great artistic talents to design the cover. Claire has sold more than 2000 prints on the Etsy online site under Operation Pumpkin.

Last, but by no means least a big thank you to my editors Andy Bates and Liz Lavender. I could not have done this without your help.

Many thanks

Paul

paul.duffin10@gmail.com

INTRODUCTION

As many people know I am a bit of a hoarder and keep things that most would throw away. I have kept my completed diaries from 1970 to 1974 which were a major part of my first book "Not Too Bad". For this book my office diaries from 1992 to 2002 were certainly of some help. They were mainly bullet points and often impossible to read due to my appalling handwriting and some of the ink fading with time.

My aim here is to bring to life some areas of my life that have left a lasting impression on me. Where appropriate, I have added some information that may be new to you.

I have tried to cover as many areas as possible and have included photos where appropriate (thank you to Andy Bates again), at the same time adding humour wherever it seemed to fit. I hope I have got the balance right and you enjoy the journey.

1. THE NATURAL WORLD

"Look deep into nature, and then you will understand everything better."

Albert Einstein

There is so much of the world I haven't seen but what I have leaves me sure old Albert was right.

The Grand Canyon (2002)

When I retired due to my sight problems in 2002 I suggested to the family that we go on a guided tour of the west side of the USA. Sue and Jenna preferred to stay in Yorkshire and embarked on their own tour, so Steve, Claire and I set off as a threesome for a 16-day coach tour adventure. We spent the first 3 days visiting the sights in Los Angeles before boarding the coach and setting off for the Grand Canyon.

We stayed for one night in the national park. It is certainly grand and very impressive. The 277 mile long canyon was created over 1000s of years by the flow of the Colorado River. It reaches a depth of one mile and exposes almost 2 billion years of the earth's geological history.

Our tour guide, a middle-aged lady called Toby, suggested we get up early to watch the sun rise over the canyon. It was a fantastic sight. The striking colours of the rock were revealed as the sun's rays lit up the sides of the canyon. We decided to have a closer look and followed a path that snaked downwards. I am not good with heights and found the uneven, unprotected, descending trail rather unsettling and soon headed back to the safety of the surface. I had dismissed the option of a flight along the canyon for the very same reason. These days there is a glass bridge for sightseers to cross. No chance!

Yosemite National Park (2002)

After the Grand Canyon we headed north stopping at Lake Tahoe, over 6000 feet above sea level. and I could feel the effect on my breathing as soon as I left the coach. The next morning, we set off for San Francisco but with no flowers in our hair. We knew we had another stop and after a while the coach pulled over. Toby declared a picture stop before entering Yosemite National Park.   The view of the valley below was magnificent. It was a truly uplifting sight that excited the whole coach for our visit. We still had quite a bit of road to travel, wending our way down into the valley below.

Toby told us to follow her to the "train" of linked open air trucks that would take us right around the valley. The whole park measures more than 1000 square miles but the valley itself is only about 7 square miles. As we got off the coach the first thing I noticed was a big sign on the bins by the cabins warning not to use them for food waste as it would attract black bears. The signs could be classed as a bare necessity!

The steep granite cliffs left by glaciers some million years ago were a fantastic sight surrounding the valley, as were the waterfalls cascading down from 3000ft above.

The whole experience left us all with huge smiles and lasting memories and a new reverence for nature.

The Great Barrier Reef (2003)

My good friend Rick Firth was keen to celebrate his 50th birthday in style with a trip to Australia, incorporating an Ashes cricket test. His wife Pam was due to go with him, but her father fell seriously ill so I was forced to step in. Well not actually forced, I was of course only too keen to help.

One slight drawback was that Rick and I would have to share a room for parts of the trip. The first night in our twin room revealed that Rick could snore for England! This was a new discovery for both Rick (as well as me) as Pam had never told him despite being together for over 20 years! It was only when I insisted that he speak to Pam on the phone that he finally accepted the truth and offered to buy me some ear plugs.

Part of our two-week trip was a few days on the lovely Hamilton Island. Whilst there we spent a memorable day sea fishing: Rick was almost launched into the ocean by the huge tuna fish on the other end of his line and I spent much of the day feeling a little seasick.

A trip out to the barrier reef was very enjoyable despite the size of the sea swell on the way there. The highlight was the organised snorkelling. It was magical to swim with fish of all sizes. Up until this point I had not had much concern for the protection of the reef but this certainly opened my eyes.

Uluru - Ayers Rock (2006)

The formation of this big red thing was almost the total opposite of Yosemite. The centre of Australia was at one time a huge sea. A massive sink hole filled with sediment and when the sea disappeared the area around it was lost leaving the big red rock behind.

You can probably tell that I was not that impressed by Uluru. However, I can appreciate it is very different and worthy of note. I think the fact that my cricket buddy Stuart and I had to fly for nearly 4 hours from Sydney as an option on our Ashes cricket tour and arrive at a place where the temperature was in the high 40s didn't help.

If it is not too windy it was possible to walk up the side of the rock with the aid of a rope to hold as you climb. Some people have fallen off and it is now prohibited. We were taken to view it at sunrise *and* sunset. Unfortunately, it was cloudy on both occasions and it was still just a big red rock. The drinks and canapes helped a little although I still wished I had opted for a couple of days in Sydney instead, before moving on to the Adelaide test match. The key lesson here was to take more time researching touring options and not falling for the sales pitch.

Mount Etna (2009)

I have always loved Italy right from my very first cornetto. Sorry, slip of the tongue. My first visit was a business trip to the computer company Olivetti in 1989 via Milan and Venice. Yes, you are right it was a "Jolly" that Sue and I enjoyed with nine others and their other halves. This trip to Sicily was made with our friends Dennis, Barbara, Dilys and Stuart.

We stayed in a very nice hotel in Taormina on the eastern side of the large island. The coastal town boasts sandy beaches accessible via a meandering path from the hilltop town. Overlooking the sea is the ancient Greek theatre Teatro Antico which was later rebuilt by the Romans and is still in use today.

We took advantage of our proximity to Mount Etna to visit this active volcano which rises to almost 11,000 feet above sea level. It was actually alarmingly active at the time. From our hotel, particularly at night, we could see the flames leaping and flaring in the darkness. We booked a guided tour and set off in a minibus. It was the middle of May but the track to the top meandered through several feet of SNOW. As we climbed out of the minibus we shivered and instantly regretted our lack of more substantial clothing. The guide took us to the edge of a crater, and we peered in. There was a worrying lack of safety. The only thing preventing us from slipping into the molten mass was a thin rope supported by equally thin metal rods. We moved around stepping very carefully. There were several craters but one was enough for most of us. I remembered seeing Mount Vesuvius from our hotel balcony in Sorrento. Mount Etna easily dwarfed it being more than twice as high and far more active.

The experience left me with a greater understanding of the power of nature and a new respect for the protection provided by the earth's "upper crust".

The Nile (2004, 2005 and 2007)

Andy and I made three trips to Egypt in the summers/spring of 2004, 2005 and 2007. On our first trip we spent four nights cruising the Nile and three nights visiting the pyramids and Cairo. The next two trips were spent entirely on the Nile. It was a great experience and 21 days with no illness. The history is incredible and the sights wonderful.

The River Nile has been the life blood of the region for thousands of years. It flows over 4000 miles from Rwanda through several countries into the Mediterranean Sea. It is thought to be the longest river in the world although some argue that the Amazon is longer. It is surprisingly shallow averaging between 26 and 36 feet. The locks are also narrow therefore the cruise ships are quite small with an average capacity of around one hundred passengers excluding crew.

The natural annual flood laid new fertile deposits to enable the Egyptians to grow and trade wheat, flax, papyrus and other crops. This gave them stability in the region. The Nile also provided an effective means of transport. The Nile was so important to the Egyptians that it entered their belief system, both literally and metaphorically representing life and death.

Completion of the Aswan High Dam (the highest embankment dam in the world) in 1970 ended the annual floods and improved water storage and irrigation. It also provided hydroelectricity. All of which led to a rise in the fortunes of the country.

There is a current dispute focusing on the building of the Grand Ethiopian Renaissance Dam on the Blue Nile. Sudan and Egypt have serious concerns over the impact of the dam on their water supplies.

I was frequently struck by the role this great river had played in the economic and cultural development of this fascinating country. There were some lighter moments such as the hilarity on board as the ships queued for the lock. A large number of small boats came up to each ship selling their wares, mostly towels, sheets and tablecloths. They were tossed up to those interested, for inspection. Not surprisingly many didn't make the decks and splashed back into the river. The locals persevered and seemed unfazed in their splash for cash. It was something to entertain us during the long wait for our turn to pass through the lock. I would love to revisit this amazing country if at all possible.

Rotorua (2008)

New Zealand boasts many examples of the power of the world that lies beneath our feet. The thermal springs at Rotorua being just one. My cricket buddy Stuart and I were trying to recover from watching England losing the test in Hamilton New Zealand the previous day. Remarkably we could smell Rotorua before we entered the town. Our destination was the Thermal Park, home to lots of hot springs, geysers and mud pools. The blowing geysers were certainly impressive, but I really didn't like the constant smell of sulphur fumes. It was just all gas and geysers to me.

Milford Sound (2008)

After the Test cricket matches in Hamilton (lost) and Wellington (won) had been completed, Stuart and I joined a small tour group that broke off from those going home and set off to visit New Zealand's South Island. Our first stop was Queenstown, which sits on the edge of a lake and is home to many outdoor adventurers.

After a couple of very enjoyable days, we set off on a five hour coach journey to Milford Sound. This striking fjord was once described by Rudyard Kipling as the 8th wonder of the world. It is exceedingly good, but I think old Mr Kipling was trying to have his cake and eat it.

The Sound is about 1000 ft at its deepest. On our visit the weather wasn't great, but the bursts of rain fed the numerous waterfalls that tumble from the cliffs around the fjord. The visit left me thinking about visiting the Scandinavian fjords to be able to compare the sights. We were supposed to fly back but the weather was considered too bad and the loss of a group of visitors in recent months made the decision a simple one.

Dunn's River Falls Jamaica (2009)

On another cricket trip, this time to Jamaica, we spent the first few days in a lovely spot on Montego Bay, where I hooked up with Richard and John who I had met on previous cricket tours.

On day 3 we travelled on to Kingston for the start of the test match. Although we were in no real hurry our coach sped through the village of Sherwood Content without stopping. This was where the sprinter Usain Bolt was born! We did stop at Dunn's River Falls for a very enjoyable climb up a waterfall.

Walking up a 900ft waterfall sounds impossible but we did it. Our group started at the beach where we received careful instructions. We were warned that despite it being a fairly gentle climb there were some steeper parts, and it was almost certain that we would fall down. We did fall down but we got up again. There was much whooping and hollering accompanied by the official video man regularly shouting, 'Yeah man". Great fun in the sun as we made it safely to the top with no broken bones.

The natural world is both fascinating and at times dangerous. I have also learnt that we humans have impacted in both good and bad ways.

2. MAN-MADE

"If you build it, they will come" …from the film Field of Dreams (1989)

Man has created some amazing structures for us to admire. Everyone will have their favourites, here are some of mine.

Eiffel Tower (1967)

In my second year at Central Grammar school my parents paid the £20 cost for my trip in weekly instalments. The week in a Paris boarding school was supposed to improve my French. It did not. What I did learn was that I have a real fear of heights.

The Eiffel Tower is only about 300 metres (984ft) tall. When it was completed in 1889 it was the tallest man-made structure in the world. I entered the lift confidently enough but as it rose with a pretty clear view through the metal gated entrance, I began to feel a little uneasy. When we reached the top and the lattice gates slid back, I was overcome with fear. I just about made it outside with my back now firmly pressed against the nearest secure support. I was terrified by what I learned later to be vertigo. The wind was blowing me backwards and I feared the tower was going to collapse. Nobody seemed to notice my reluctance to move as they were enjoying an *eye full* of the sights. I was the first back in the lift and made sure I didn't look as we descended.

Despite my vertigo I really was taken by the look of the tower being so different to any of the surrounding buildings and structures.

The tower wasn't that popular when built to mark the entrance to the World's Fair, but now it is regarded as iconic and visited by up to 7 million people a year. I liked the look of it so much so that when I returned there to celebrate my friend Andy's 40th birthday (1994) we went up as far as the first floor where I could enjoy a nice cup of coffee and be a long way from the edge.

Statue of Liberty (1997)

I should have known better but I thought my fear of heights would not surface when sat securely in the middle of three seats at the back of the helicopter. After all I did not suffer at all on aircraft which I considered "plane sailing'.

It was great to visit New York on business and my colleague Andy McLoughlin was keen to fly along the Hudson River to get a good view of the statue donated by the French in 1886.

I was OK for about the first 30 seconds. As soon as we left the ground the whole body started to move around. It was worse when we moved along the river. We circled the Statue of Liberty which looked much smaller from the air than I expected. I clung on for dear life trying not to make the other passengers on either side be aware of my fears. I can understand why people arriving many years ago would have been both impressed and relieved to know they had arrived with the prospect of a new free life.

We had paid extra to add Central Park to our flight. 'Why did we do that?' I asked myself. This was before the TV "Friends" had started so at least we didn't swoop down for a close view of "Central Perk" the coffee shop featured in the series.

I was so relieved to get both feet back on the ground and thankful that Andy, my colleague, was unaware of my discomfort. We were greeted with some good news. Our boss Dick Spelman had wisely ducked out of the trip but had arranged an evening meal at an exclusive restaurant. He had been able to get us a reservation via our advertising agent's New York office. Dick had eaten there before and promised us a pleasant surprise.

The 21 Club opened in 1922 and moved to its current location in 1929. It had an old club feel with the strange addition of painted cast iron lawn racehorse jockeys. More than a little odd but they were gifts from satisfied customers. It was a speakeasy during the Prohibition, and it felt at times that we were due a raid at any moment. After an excellent meal and splendid wine Dick announced that we were going to move to see our surprise. A staff member led us to a wall and amazingly swung open a completely hidden door so smoothly despite its size. It revealed a room with wine bottles lining all the walls. In the centre was a dining table with about 20 places.

The staff member explained that this was where people hid when a raid occurred during the Prohibition. You could now hire the room for private meals, and you could store your own supply of wine. He told us that many famous people had kept their wine there over the years including Richard Nixon, Marilyn Monroe, Sinatra. Sammy Davis Jnr and Elizabeth Taylor. He showed us the wine collection of the current Mayor of New York, Giuliani. It was a fascinating surprise.

Sydney Harbour Bridge (2003)

What do you buy the man who has almost everything? It was Rick's 50th birthday and he should really have been accompanied by his wife Pam, not me. I asked him what he wanted to do on his special day. He didn't hesitate and came straight out with "fly over Sydney harbour bridge in a helicopter". "My treat" was my instant reply.

I know what you are thinking but I was so grateful for being there and we had had such a great time. I would just have to grin and bear it.

I did just that. I took up the exact same position as I did in New York. Middle of the back row of three. We took off from the outskirts of Sydney airport and were soon flying in between the tall office buildings. Rick was sat in the front next to the pilot and had the spare headphones on so he could hear everything the pilot said. He could also hear the control tower. I was doing quite well until we reached the harbour bridge. We went over it smoothly but suddenly we zoomed upwards at fast speed. Apparently, a sea plane was landing in the harbour and we were being taken out of its path. The pilot was not at all concerned but I was. Things soon returned to normal and the main thing was that I could see how much Rick had enjoyed it. As we stepped out, he shook my hand and thanked me enthusiastically.

The bridge was opened in 1932. On an average day 200 trains and 160,000 cars will cross over it. You can pay to climb the structure's 440 feet. Many tourists take that route but not this one. Just nice to admire it with both feet firmly on the ground.

Sydney Opera House (2003)

Yes, it is an odd shape from the outside. It was also very odd on the inside with lots of areas sectioned off like wooden stalls. We bought tickets to see the only thing on at the time. An Italian opera sung not surprisingly in Italian. Not until near the end did I notice the English words on the moving screen high above the stage. I am sure Rick nodded off during the performance, but he denied it. At least he didn't snore.

From the outside it is very striking and can be seen from most parts of the city.

The residential flats next to it did not prove popular when constructed and were labelled as "the toast rack" due to their similarity to the kitchen accessory. It didn't put Michael Parkinson off buying one at the time.

The Colosseum (2003)

I chose to visit Italy for my 50th birthday splitting the week between Rome and Sorrento. The striking thing about Rome is that there is history on every street. At least that's how it felt to me. Sue and I visited all the main attractions except for the Sistine Chapel which was closed for repairs. Probably a paint job.

Our hotel was close to the Colosseum which is the largest amphitheatre ever built. It is still in pretty good condition over 2000 years later, especially considering the damage caused by earthquakes and people removing stonework for their own use. At its peak it could hold c65,000 people.

We paid to join a tour group and were taken around the parts open to the public. It was impressive and the guide brought the battles fought by the gladiators to life. You could almost hear the roar of both the crowd and the animals. We had such a good time we paid to go on the afternoon tour of the Forum situated nearby run by students. Still plenty left to see and lots of ice cream treats left behind as we went up Pompeii.

Pompeii (2003)

As it was my 50th birthday we treated ourselves to a four day stay in the lovely hotel Victoria right in the centre of Sorrento. Our room had a balcony overlooking the Bay of Naples with Vesuvius lurking in the background.

We opted for an organised trip to the ruins of Pompeii. The guide was excellent bringing alive the city devastated 2000 years ago when Vesuvius violently erupted burying the city and many of its inhabitants in hot ash and lava. Many of the streets and buildings have been brought out of the debris enabling visitors to experience a return to how it was. Shops can be identified, as can other important buildings. Graffiti and paintings can be found along with instructions such as "Cave Canem"(beware of the dog).

Pompeii was the main city in the area but some of the wealthier people had houses close to the sea at Herculaneum. We visited the equally impressive smaller site a few years later.

If you are interested, Robert Harris's book "Pompeii" is an interesting blend of fact and fiction. Well worth a read. I am a little biased as I am a Harris fan.

The Pyramids (2004)

Andy and I stayed 3 nights at the Mena House hotel overlooking the Pyramids at Giza near Cairo. We weren't the first celebrities (ha ha) to stay there as Churchill met Roosevelt in 1943 and Roger Moore was housed there whilst filming "The Spy Who Loved Me". We expected to be impressed by the pyramids and we were not disappointed. They were right next to the hotel but we still had to board a coach just to cross the road. It was probably a security issue or may just have been a way of helping with local employment.

I had no intention of going inside the Great Pyramid due to my fear, not of heights this time, but of claustrophobia. In addition to the Great Pyramid there were two other large ones a few small ones that could be easily retreated from. I had a quick look around one of the Queens pyramids. It was one of the smaller ones that was open and it gave me a feel for their design. The scale of the main ones was incredible and how on earth they were constructed is still the subject of some debate amongst the experts. The original limestone outer covering had been removed much later probably to construct other buildings in nearby Cairo.

Terracotta Warriors (2011)

Andy and I had a fantastic trip visiting the main sites in China on an organised Jules Verne tour. I could mention lots of places but settled on the two that really stood out.

The Terracotta Army is without doubt one of the greatest archaeological finds of the 20th century and it blew me away. If you go to China, you really must visit this incredible site and take in the 8000 life size statues. Each one is different in some way, such as an expression or a gesture.

The amazing afterlife army was built for the Emperor about 250BC. It took over 700,00 labourers about 40 years to complete. It is not just soldiers as there are 130 chariots and

670 horses. There are also acrobats, musicians and even birds.

There are three main halls covering the army of warriors below. The impact on entering the main hall was staggering. The army were in rows below ground level and we could walk around the whole arena. They were still working on the statues at the rear. There were smaller displays of horses and chariots that we could view closely.

Its discovery in 1974 was both amazing and fortunate. Found by local farmers who were digging for a well, had they dug just a few feet to one side they would have gone past the very end of the site and it may have not been uncovered for many years. When we visited, one of the farmers was sat signing his book about the amazing discovery. I didn't buy one despite really "digging" the whole experience.

Some have deemed it the eighth wonder of the world, it would certainly be in my top ten.

Great Wall of China (2011)

I am not sure how many official entrances there are to the Great Wall. The one chosen for us meant a long uphill walk past gift stall after gift stall, each with enthusiastic sellers promoting their goods. It was a bit of a pain and took some of the magic away until we actually got on to the wall itself.

It was just how I had imagined it having seen it plenty of times on TV. It still had a magical feel as the pathway on top of the wall rolled into the distance in both directions, weaving its way across the landscape occasionally interrupted by watch towers.

We climbed lots of steps up and down the wall. They were there so we had to travel along the wall for a while and then head back. My daughter Claire was a big fan of the American TV series "Trauma". It had been cancelled after the end of the first season and there was uproar from fans across the world.

A campaign was launched to raise awareness and force the show back for a second season. People were having their picture taken lying on the floor in the recovery position, the more interesting the background the better. As Claire had instructed, I lay on the floor while Andy snapped away. The picture turned out well, but despite the huge campaign the show did not return.

The wall was first built at roughly the same time as the Terracotta Army under the same emperor. In the early days it was mainly earth and wood. Brick and stones replaced the crude wall in the Ming dynasty and the wall has had many others put another brick in the wall along its 11,000 mile route.

We humans are guilty of damaging our world but have also repeatedly demonstrated an incredible ability to create lasting evidence of skill, design and innovation.

3. INTERESTING PLACES AROUND LONDON

"By seeing London, I have seen as much of life as the world can show".

Samuel Johnson

An advantage of working at the Halifax was the opportunity to go to some interesting places and meet some fascinating people.

10 and 11 Downing Street

One day back in the summer of 1998 totally out of the blue my boss at the Halifax Mike Ellis summoned me to his office. That was not unusual, but on arrival he led me to the opposite office where CEO James Crosby was sat beckoning us in. He then asked me if I would like to go to the Prime Minister's office to represent the Halifax at a meeting regarding a new savings initiative. I was tempted to say, "is the Pope Catholic?" or "do bears………?" I just said I would be delighted.

The next day I arrived at the police booth at the end of Downing Street, confidently waved my ID at the officer and marched up to the famous black door, which 100 years ago was apparently green. I was greeted by a very friendly lady armed with a clipboard who took me inside. The iconic staircase which appears regularly on television was right there in front of me and I took my time to view the portraits of previous prime ministers as I walked up to the offices above.

The building was like Dr Who's Tardis. At the top we entered a surprisingly huge meeting room where chairs were laid out for probably 50 or more people with most of them already occupied. This was not going to be the cosy chat around the table I was expecting. PM Tony Blair and Chancellor Alastair Darling marched in with a couple of assistants and sat at the table facing the rest of us. Blair was confident and firmly in charge. Darling was also professional, but I couldn't take my eyes off those eyebrows. "Don't call him "Darling", I thought, with my mind rushing back to Captain Darling in the "Blackadder Goes Forth" comedy.

The Government were proposing a trial of a savings initiative to help encourage non-savers to adopt the savings habit. I immediately thought "nice idea but unlikely to work". As Halifax were the largest provider of savings and it was part of my responsibility, I knew we would have to volunteer to take part and of course we did. Despite best efforts, and for obvious reasons (such as lack of funds), the scheme bombed and was quietly dropped. Half the population had no savings and offering them a small amount of cash was not going to change that.

A year or so later I returned to Downing Street, this time to visit number 11. This was a much more low-key affair, so much so that my memories of the visit have faded considerably. I suspect it is partly due to having been so excited by my previous visit.

I can remember having a cup of tea and chatting to the MP Patricia Hewitt who at the time was Economic Secretary to the Treasury. She was keen to tell me she had an account with the Halifax. I think the Treasury civil servant Paula Diggle was also there so it must have been linked to my responsibility for mortgages.

Number 11 is merged with both number 10 and number 12 (Whip's office) and the whole area has been expanded to over 100 rooms. Although the PM's accommodation is normally above number 10, our current PM (Boris Johnson) is using the much more spacious facilities above number 11 as have several past PM's including Blair and Cameron.

The resident cat at number 10 and 11 is "Larry the mouser". He is a rescue cat thought to be about 13 yrs old (in 2020). Not sure how current PM Boris gets on with Larry but David Cameron told the press their relationship was "Purrfect.

The House of Lords

In May 1999 the Labour Government was keen to make improvements to the house buying process. It considered the system too slow and on occasions allowed Gazumping (out bidding). There were suggestions that the Scottish bidding system should be considered. As a result, several representatives of the largest mortgage lenders were invited to dinner at the House of Lords to discuss the issue.

I enjoyed the experience as far as the location and the food and drink was concerned. The discussion was poor as it was fairly obvious that the powers that be were determined to be seen to do something. Yet again as Halifax was the largest lender, we were asked to support a trial of the proposed improvement. We pointed out the weaknesses of the "Home Information Pack" but we were obliged to take part. The packs showed up severe weaknesses, but it was eventually introduced in 2009. After much criticism it was withdrawn by the incoming government in 2010. On average a purchase takes more than 3 months from when the offer is accepted, a very stressful process that still needs attention.

The Palace of Westminster

It came as a very pleasant surprise when I was invited by The British Heart Foundation to make a speech at the Parliament building. Prior to being taken over by the Halifax the Leeds Permanent Building Society launched a charity credit card. Three charities were available for customers to choose from: Cancer Research, Mind and the British Heart Foundation (BHF).

I was delighted to accept the invitation to speak on our support of the BHF. I was not going to stand and deliver at the dispatch box in the House itself. The BHF function was to take place on the terrace overlooking the Thames complete with marquee in case of bad weather.

I was accompanied by Carolyn Holroyd who was responsible for Marketing. I found it easy to talk fondly of BHF because of my experience of losing both my father and brother in their 40's to heart conditions. Afterwards Carolyn and I walked out of the building and decided to find somewhere to eat. We soon discovered that the area around Westminster is bereft of restaurants. We were just deciding what to do when the former ASDA CEO MP Archie Norman came striding along the pavement. I politely asked him if he could recommend somewhere but he said we would need to head towards Soho. (Soho we did). I nearly said "there ASDA be somewhere" but wisely thought better of it.

Archie Norman moved on to become Chairman of Marks & Spencer. He was previously Chairman of ITV becoming the first person to be a FTSE 100 chairman and an MP at the same time.

HM Treasury

In 1998 I was invited by the cabinet office to take part in a government task force to review Credit Unions (CU's). A Credit Union is a member-owned financial cooperative run by its members, helping them to receive competitive rates and other financial services. They offer products to people often left behind by traditional financial institutions.

I wasn't a member of the task force for very long as I moved roles from Banking General Manager (GM) to Mortgages and Savings GM soon after. However, I do have some interesting memories. The Treasury building was located in Horse Guards Road. The Treasury building was well overdue refurbishment. Built at the beginning of the 20th century, not much had changed since the Treasury took over the building in 1940. There were cables strewn everywhere and it looked more like a prison than a vital instrument of government.

The other task force members included representatives of some of the larger CU's and a very impressive Treasury civil servant who was always keen to explain technicalities and guide us in the right direction.

Probably the most memorable person was the man appointed as our chairman. Fred Goodwin had just been appointed deputy CEO at the Royal Bank of Scotland after leaving his position as CEO at National Australia Bank. He was known in the City as "Fred the Shred" due to his reputation for cost cutting. He was an effective chairman with no sign of the controlling personality he was later credited with. He may have been inclined to be very engaging in a role outside his normal sphere of influence. He was later awarded a knighthood which he then handed back. An honour he chose to *shred*.

I never met him again but heard quite a lot about him. After I retired, I did some business coaching for Tony Brown who moved from HBOS (Halifax Bank of Scotland) to RBS (Royal Bank of Scotland). Just after he joined RBS Tony attended a management conference. Fred suddenly asked Tony to stand up in the middle of a crowded arena and explain to everyone present why HBOS seemed to be doing so well. It was apparently not unusual for Goodwin to pick out people and Tony managed to handle the challenge.

RBS expanded rapidly under Goodwin, but it all came to an abrupt end during the financial crisis in 2008.

It is said that Goodwin hated mess and even introduced filing cabinets with sloping tops in his 20-metre square penthouse office so that nothing would look untidy on top of them. The slide had begun.

Hever Castle, Kent

During my stint heading up Banking I joined the board of VISA UK as did a number of representatives from other banks. It was not a very demanding role as my main duty was to attend board meetings and comment as necessary. The major highlight was the board's two-day strategy meeting at Hever Castle in Kent.

The castle was built in 1270 but is best known as the home of Henry VIII's second wife Anne Boleyn. It later fell into decline until it was taken over by the Astor family around 1900 who spent a fortune restoring the castle and adding the impressive "Tudor Village".

I can't remember a thing about the meeting itself, but the castle stands out in my memory. The meeting was held in the Great Hall. One of the ornate locks is the original fitted for Henry who was a regular visitor and being very fearful of assassination he insisted on tight security. We were given a guided tour and found that many of the rooms had furniture that dated back to the 16th century. Anne Boleyn's room had some of her possessions. There was a huge heavily structured bed in the room thought to have been used by King Henry. Let's face it Henry was a big chap and would need plenty of support.

To sleep in the castle's amazing atmosphere was a real privilege. As usual I slept like a log but woke up finding it hard to believe where I was. It was a truly magical experience.

Somerset House

Located on the Strand in the centre of London the original house was built in 1549. Queen Elizabeth I lived there for 5 years before she was crowned in 1558. The original building was demolished in 1775 and rebuilt and extended over the years with many different uses. In 1836 the General Registry for births, marriages and deaths moved in and stayed until 1970. It is now a centre for the Arts. It has an impressive courtyard that becomes the home of an impressive outdoor ice rink from November to January.

When I retired due to my sight problems in 2002 I was able to stay on the board of the HBOS Foundation. The foundations awards functions were held each year to celebrate the outstanding work and fund raising achieved by the HBOS staff. They were great nights and celebrities were often invited to host the evening. One such event was held at Somerset House and hosted by the late Bruce Forsyth. He was extremely professional and word perfect. The audience loved him. My only criticism was his huge fee despite it being his reduced "charity fee". He certainly knew how to "Play his Cards Right". I am not sure "The Price Is Right", but it was nice to see him.

After Sir Bruce passed away in 2017 his ashes were laid to rest behind the stage at the London Palladium. This was where he came to fame presenting ITV's Sunday Night at the London Palladium in the mid- 1950's.

4. THE ENGLISH SEASON

"Eat, drink and be merry while the sun shines"

Anon

A hundred years ago "the Season" was the time when the great and the good travelled to London to enjoy the social events of the spring and summer. They would then retreat to their country piles for the winter months. These days it is seen as attending some of the major events of the spring and summer. Sue and I have had some great times with good friends attending some, but not all of those listed by "The Sloaney Season".

Cheltenham Festival (March)

The Season kicks off with this huge horse racing event held around St Patrick's day (17th) in the middle of March attracting many visitors from the emerald isle. The prize money on offer at the four-day event is second only to the Grand National. The big race is the Cheltenham Gold Cup.

Although I'm not a keen follower of horse racing, I do enjoy a good day out. I attended the Cheltenham Festival on two separate occasions. The first was in the late 80's with my good friend Rick Firth. This was an organised trip from our local pub, The Swan in Holmes Chapel Cheshire. It started with a coach load of guys having an early breakfast in the pub with Peter the landlord who organised the trip. The Festival attracts around a quarter of a million visitors over the whole event and when we arrived it was packed. I can't remember if I had any winners, but Rick still recalls celebrating a win with "Pearly Man". It was an enjoyable day until we stopped for fish and chips at a pub on the way home. Unbeknown to me there was some "adult entertainment" for us to 'enjoy' after we had eaten. I am not a prude, but I felt really uncomfortable as a couple of ladies strutted their stuff and dangled their wobbly bits! I pulled the table in front of me as close as I could hoping it would provide sufficient protection. It did and I survived.

The second trip to Cheltenham was rather different. In 2006 I was invited to join my old friends Martin Wood and Steve Clayton at the races. They were regular attenders and still are. I was delighted when Martin said he had an old university friend who was going and could pick me up as he lived not too far away from me. When his friend Paul arrived, I was surprised to see there were two people sat in the front of the car. A hand emerged from the passenger door and pointed to the back seat. I settled in and it soon became apparent that Paul had hired a driver. How posh, I thought at first but before long I realised this was going to be a long journey. Paul was an odd chap who demonstrated the social skills of a "brick" (I nearly wrote something else!) He was not at all friendly and left the driver in no doubt that he was just "staff". During the day the Guinness flowed with many Irish visitors really enjoying the black stuff. I decided to be cautious as I had to face a 300 mile return trip with the "brick". I kept very quiet on the return trip and was very glad that I had not been tempted to join the boys with black stuff.

On 17th March 1987 Gee Armytage became the first female jockey to win a race at the Festival. She won again the very next day. During the Covid outbreak the Festival was still held with the usual 250,000 visitors. There was a lot of criticism of it being held and many people contracted the virus including my friend Steve Clayton. The World Health Organisation declared the outbreak of the virus a pandemic on the second day of the festival (11th March 2020). Three days *after* the Festival the Government banned large gatherings. The timing of the Festival was very unfortunate and caused quite a controversy.

The Grand National (April)

The next event on the Season's calendar is the Grand National at Aintree in Liverpool. I made two visits. The first was in April 1987 as a guest of Barratts the house builders. The day started with breakfast, this time in a Manchester hotel, then a coach to Aintree. Barratts gave us all some cash to place a bet which, being a wise soul, I donated the whole amount to charity. I made sure I had a receipt which I kept for a very long time. At the course we had the Liverpudlian comedian Stan ("they bombed our chip shop") Boardman standing in the middle of our group entertaining us and others in the crowd between races. I don't know if his chip shop really was bombed in the war, but sadly when he returned from being evacuated, he discovered his elder brother had been killed in a bombing raid. It was a long day with some lighter moments, but it was still work.

Two years later a group of friends from Mallaig Close in Holmes Chapel where we were living at the time decided to plan our own outing to Aintree. We packed hampers of food and drink in our car boots and set off in a convoy. It was fun and rewarding when out of sheer frustration I put £10 on the horse with the longest odds in the very last race. Jenny Pitman's Vazon Bay won at 33/1. I am not a regular gambler and that was my best win until Danny Willett won the 2016 Masters Golf at 66/1. The win ruined his game for a long time but I still place small bets on all four golf majors and am still well ahead of the bookies. This was much more fun than the earlier trip. More relaxed with good friends.

It is estimated that between 500 and 600 million people across 140 countries watch the race each year. During the First World War the race was transferred to Gatwick racecourse. No longer in use it has now been swallowed up by Gatwick airport. In the Second World War the race was not held from 1941 to 1945.

The biggest drawback of the event is the risk to both horses and jockeys that the very challenging, tough course presents.

Royal Ascot (June)

This was a lovely day out for Sue and I. Sue is not a great lover of hats and was grateful to borrow a really nice one from our friend and neighbour Cathy MacDougall. I think it was American Express who invited us. We were located in a very posh marquee very close to the finishing line. During a splendid meal a couple of racing experts (husband and wife) went through the whole card. They gave us lots of background knowledge and really seemed to know what they were talking about.

We didn't have to go far to place a bet as the Tote had a counter in the marquee. We placed our bets and went a few yards to the finishing post. As the races came and went so did our money. The experts did not pick a single winner. It was a good job we only placed a small amount on each race. We left without a win but with huge smiles after a great day.

Nearly £8 million in prize money is competed for during the five days of racing by around 500 horses. 20,000 flowers and shrubs are specially grown for the event.

As it is a flat race the danger to both horse and jockey is far less than the Grand National

Lords Test Match (June)

I love cricket and have travelled the world watching England play. It wasn't until June 1980 that I sat in the Mound stand at the home of cricket for the first time. I was the Leeds PB Society branch manager in Bridgwater Somerset and was there with one of our valuers from Taunton, a lovely guy called David Ware.

I enjoyed watching Graham Gooch hit a century against the very quick West Indies bowlers including Holding and Garner. The sun didn't shine but my face still got burnt sat in the open with the sun half out. The ground is really more impressive when visited than it is on TV. A full house provides a fantastic atmosphere. We all stood when Gooch reached his century and "oohed and aahed" as the pace bowlers peppered the batsmen.

A very enjoyable day that was followed by many visits to test matches around the world (contained in my book "And the cricket was good too").

Cricket is not the only game to have been played at Lords. During World War 1 a baseball game was played in front of 10,000 to raise money for a Canadian widows and orphans fund. In 1967 a couple of pre-Olympics hockey games were played including a very competitive match between Pakistan and India with Pakistan beating their rivals 1-0. During the 2012 Olympics the Archery was held at the ground.

Wimbledon Tennis Championships (June/July)

I have never been a very good tennis player even before I developed problems with my eyesight. I played for fun and a bit like my cricket I tended to be very defensive. My dad was a very good player who served with one hand and played his ground strokes with the other. He won quite a few local tournaments and managed to break his arm when he unsuccessfully tried to vault the net at the end of winning a final.

Sue and I had always liked the idea of going to Wimbledon. The thought of strawberries and ice cream followed by something fizzy appealed to us both, as it did to our good friends Barbara and Dennis Skinner. Over a tasty Thai curry at Yum Yum in Wetherby we decided to book a package which included food, drink and tickets.

We chose the cheapest day at the 2013 tournament which surprisingly was ladies semi-final day on the Thursday of the second week. In the end we did not see the ladies semis played but we had tickets to number one court to see the men's doubles semi-final. The marquee was beautifully decked out as we arrived. We were the first there and had coffee and nibbles and read the papers. We quickly moved on to the pre-lunch drinks. The choice was extensive, naturally we settled for champers, determined to enjoy the day and get our money's worth.

The marquee was situated on the golf course immediately opposite the main entrance to the All England Club. There were golf carts to take us back and forwards even though it was only a couple of hundred yards. We took our seats on court number one and watched the Bryan Brothers cruise to the final. We did all the things we planned to include. Strawberries and ice cream and champers were consumed. We strolled around the outside courts and breathed in the atmosphere the crowd brought to the event. We had a great time enjoying every minute.

Wimbledon has seen many changes over the years. Black players were not allowed to play at the club until 1951 and Jews banned from being members until 1952. Equal prize money was introduced in 2007. The delay was blamed on men playing the best of five sets as opposed to ladies playing the best of only three. In 2003 the practice of bowing to the Royal box was discontinued unless the Queen was in attendance.

Henley Royal Regatta (July)

We had such a good time at Wimbledon that the four of us looked for a similar event in 2014. We settled on the Henley Royal Regatta. None of us had the slightest interest in rowing, however the same sporting hospitality firm were offering a similar package for Henley. As with Wimbledon we went for the cheapest complete package.

The only problem was getting there from our base in centre of London. No one wanted to drive for obvious reasons. We looked at taxis, but it was a long way out of the centre of London. We settled on the train. We took a strange route and we had to make a change and then walk a long way to our hospitality venue. We were near to the bandstand and not far from the finishing line. Did we watch the rowing? They raced, we drank and ate. We had no idea what was going on. It was a lovely sunny day and the band played on. We sat very comfortably by the river, glass in hand and didn't give a damn.

Following the course being shortened in the early 1980's, women competitors entered the event. Henley hosted the rowing events for the 1908 Olympics. They missed out at the 2012 Olympics when the rowing was held at Dorney Lake.

It was along walk back to the station with the tow path crowded with happy, tipsy people. Unfortunately, with my sight and hearing continuing to deteriorate it was the last trip of that kind.

Edinburgh Festival (August)

I went to the lovely Scottish city many times when working for HBOS. Our Head Office was situated on the Mound where the old Bank of Scotland had ruled for many a year before being swallowed by the Halifax in 2001.

My first visit to the "Fringe" was with our daughter Claire in 2006. She wanted to research female stand-up comedians for her dissertation, and I was happy to accompany her. We watched lots of them, including Sue Perkins. We also saw a couple of chaps to add some balance. It was great fun and made me want to return.

Two years later I was back with Sue and our good friends Pam and Rick Firth. They stayed with their friends Carol and Mike who were living in the city at the time. We saw some very different shows. From a weird play about a nuclear attack, to amusing performances from Andy Parsons and Paul Merton. Our hotel was in a great spot, handy for everything in a packed town centre.

The Fringe usually has more than 300 different venues for over 3000 events. It is often used by performers to try out or improve routines. In 2012 comedian Michael McIntyre was criticised for charging £31 for a "work in progress" Show. The same year Harry Hill only charged £15 for his "work in progress" show. Mind you who would you rather see?

The events that got away

Boat Race (April)

This race has no real significance unless you are connected to Oxford or Cambridge. I admit I used to watch it on TV when I was young for two main reasons. Apart from Test cricket and the Cup Final there was little else in the way of live sport other than wrestling, horse racing and old-style rugby league. Secondly, I wanted to see one of the boats sink which did happen very occasionally. It was a bit like watching the first lap of F1 hoping for a pile up, with no one hurt of course. The good news is that it only takes less than 20 minutes to row from Mortlake to Putney.

The Epsom Derby (June)

"No more horse racing" I hear you cry. Ok let's move on.

Chelsea Flower show (May)

Can't face water features as my prostate may overreact. Not into gardening and there appears to be little to do except perhaps have a nice cup of tea.

Badminton Horse Trials (May)

No one is ever found guilty at these trials except me when I want them to fall at those huge fences and ditches, without injury of course.

End of Season

5. BACK TO BRUM

"I grew up in Birmingham where they made useful things and made them well".

Author Lee Child

If you have read any of my previous books particularly "Not Too Bad" or 'When I was Lad in Brum" you will know I was born in Aston Birmingham in 1953, a baby booming Brummie. We moved to the suburb of Yardley a year later. I look back with pride and pleasure at a wonderful upbringing. Being part of a loving family in a friendly and caring neighbourhood I was so lucky. Only 3 miles from the city centre we had access to all essential services and entertainments. The population is now over one million.

Parks

Living near to the Yew Tree in Yardley I could walk to 3 parks within about 10 minutes. The Oaklands park was also very close to Hobmoor Primary school which I attended from 1958 to 1965. It was the ground where we played football and cricket against other schools and held our annual sports day. My speciality was the potato race. About 4 potatoes were spaced out in a straight line and we had to race along to pick each one and return to place them in a basket. I called it the King Edwards chase

I remember marching up Hobmoor Croft with the other pupils behind Mr Hughes, my Stanley Matthews boots tied together and draped around my neck. I no longer have those boots but I still have the card signed by Matthews that came with them. He was knighted in 1965 whilst still playing for Stoke City. The only footballer to be made a Sir whilst still playing.

Because Yardley is one of the highest areas in the city you could see the tall buildings in the centre 3 miles away from the edge of the Oaklands park.

Queen's Road park was next to the parish church and had a couple of proper football pitches that I appeared on a few times. Finally, there was "Gilbertstone Rec" that we called Moat Lane mainly because it was situated on Moat Lane. It had a couple of tennis courts that we would flock to when Wimbledon made us search for our racquets. How lucky we were to have all these parks close at hand.

Birmingham has 571 public open spaces covering a total of 14 sq miles. This is more than any other European city. The 3 most formal areas are Cannon Hill Park, the Botanical Gardens, both located in Edgbaston, and Sutton Park.

Canals

Birmingham has 35 miles of canals which is said to be more than Venice! It also has more supermarket trollies in them and definitely fewer gondolas. My friend Alan Horton was keen on fishing and when I was about 13 he took me fishing on the canal. It was so cold we had to break the ice on the water. Not surprisingly the fish stayed well away from our lines. I never took my rod out again.

Not long after I had started work at Wragge & Co solicitors a group of us including John Clegg, John Lavender and Michael O'Mahoney ventured to canal basin in the centre of town just off Broad Street. It was Michael's 21st birthday and to celebrate we booked dinner at King Arthur's Court for a medieval banquet. The mead flowed faster than the canal and we ate everything with a spoon. We came out and ran around town playing "tig" and shouting, "Mr Spoon". We knew how to enjoy ourselves.

Off the rails

St Philips Cathedral is situated between Colmore Row and Temple Row. It had a very low wall around its perimeter. When built it also had iron railings but during the Second World War they were cut down leaving a small piece of iron in the concrete below. It was part of the war effort to provide scrap metal to be turned into weapons or parts for tanks or aeroplanes. Pots and pans were also collected from households. I can remember walking around the cathedral perimeter as a child and asking my mom what had happened to the railings. She told me about the war collections. I have since discovered that little, if any, of the metal found its way into weapons. It was a public relations exercise to help raise morale by "us all doing our bit". The churchyard railings were replaced during major works in 2001.

On the rails

There are 3 railway stations in the centre of the city: New Street (New St), Snow Hill (S.Hill) and Moor Street (MSt). All are within reasonable walking distance of each other. By far the busiest is New St with 13 platforms and over 47 million passengers in 2019 as opposed to 3 platforms and 7 million at MSt and 2 platforms and 5 million at S.Hill. I still pass through the station and although it has changed substantially over the years I still feel very much at home there.

S. Hill is the oldest, opening in 1852 with New St opening two years later in 1854. S. Hill closed in 1972 and was demolished in 1977. It was then rebuilt and opened again in 1987. MSt opened in 1909. To enable HS2 to land, a new station is being developed in Curzon Street and will be the first new intercity terminus in Britain since the 19th century. When the new station is fully operational it should significantly cut journey times to many major cities, as well as create new jobs and around 4000 new homes.

I have used all of the stations regularly but still find it a bit of a pain getting off at New St and then having to find my way out of the huge station and locate my way with my white stick to MSt to catch a train to my daughter's home in Leamington Spa. I nearly always have to stop someone for directions and have been led in the wrong direction more than once. It is surprising that it seems people can't understand me as I can speak the lingo "alright".

Cadbury

Cadbury was founded by John Cadbury in 1824. He started selling tea, coffee and chocolate drinks in the centre of Birmingham. His son George developed the Bournville estate to house workers from the Cadbury factory. It remains a desirable and popular place to live.

The Bournville factory was opened in 1879. It is still both producing and researching with over 1000 employees. The dark chocolate bar is named after the location.

I have always loved their chocolate particularly Dairy Milk and the Creme eggs. Dairy Milk was launched in the early 1900's and Creme Eggs in 1963, originally under the brand of Fry's, then re-branded to Cadburys in 1971. Taking steroids has led to type 2 diabetes so regrettably no more Cadbury's chocolate for me.

The Bournville site also houses "Cadbury World", a leisure facility describing the history of the firm and its products. We took our three children there many years ago. We all enjoyed touring and discovering the fourteen zones but at the end we were "flaked" out.

Peaky Blinders

It is difficult to mention Birmingham these days without mentioning the extremely popular BBC show. It is centred on the Shelby gang in the early 1900's. Apparently there was a similar gang in real life. The writer and creator Steven Knight has said that he wants the series to continue up to the first air raid in Birmingham in WW2 which was on 25th June 1940. The good news for followers is that he thinks this means 3 more series.

Car production

Birmingham is well known for car production at Longbridge. There were also factories at Hay Mills (Rootes Group, their cars included the Hillman, Sunbeam and Humber brands).

Longbridge opened in 1905 and other than during the two world wars, cars were built there until 2016. It was home to the Austin 7 and the Mini, followed by Rovers and MGs. At its peak it had over 25,000 employees. It is now an area of substantial regeneration.

In the 1960's a car worker's average salary increased dramatically partly due to strike action led by "Red Robbo". I can remember my dad expressing his view of how unfair it was as he earned nothing like the car workers. Many of our neighbours worked in the industry so they were quite happy.

The Rotunda

Probably the most famous building in Birmingham is The Rotunda. It was originally built as office accommodation. Nowadays it is primarily 232 apartments and a serviced aparthotel.

Construction started in 1961 and was completed in 1965. It was refurbished between 2004 and 2008. The original design included a revolving restaurant and a cinema, but they were dropped due to budget restraints. When it opened there were shops on the first two floors and a Lloyds Bank. It became a grade II listed building in August 2000. I think it now looks a little dated standing next to the modernised Bull Ring shopping centre featuring the amazing Selfridges building.

One of my memories of the Rotunda was The Mulberry Bush pub in the basement and ground floor. I had been in it a couple of times before it was hit by the pub bombings in November 1974. The other pub attacked was The Tavern situated just around the corner in New Street and a far more regular venue for young Duffin and friends.

NEC

The huge National Exhibition Centre was built close to Birmingham airport in the early 1970's. I know this because I helped build it. Whilst working at Wragge & Co I started working on site on Saturday mornings with my friend and colleague John Clegg. We were offered the work through another friend and colleague at Wragge & Co Mike O'Mahoney whose dad employed labourers for the site. Our lack of labouring skills was soon uncovered when we were asked to lay some huge piping and were unceremoniously ejected.

I have returned on a few occasions, once with Sue and friends to see Dire Straits perform. It had been a while since I had seen a major live band and could hardly believe the advances that had been made in sound quality. Mark Knopfler was outstanding, a real talent.

During the Covid19 pandemic one of its halls was prepared for overflow admissions. It was later put on standby to open at 48 hours' notice as a Nightingale hospital. If required, it could be expanded from the original 496 beds to 2000.

There is little doubt that the NEC has brought both business and pleasure to the city. Its proximity to both the airport and railway station also makes it extremely accessible.

Birmingham is a city with a great past and a promising future. I am proud to be a Brummie despite leaving me with a less than attractive accent. *Tara-a-bit, (goodbye for now).*

6. CATHEDRALS

"I went to look at one of these great cathedrals one day and was blown away by it. I then became interested in how they were built and the society that built them.'

(Author Ken Follett who wrote the popular Kingsbridge series about the construction of a cathedral)

I have always been struck by the scale of work involved in the construction and the time needed to complete each one. The craftmanship is also inspiring.

Cologne

We went on an enjoyable Rhine cruise in 2007 with our friends Dennis, Barbara, Stuart and Dilys.
We stopped off at lots of different places including Cologne in north west Germany. We were guided around the catholic cathedral; a substantial Gothic building declared a world heritage site in 1996. It is Germany's most visited site with thousands of visitors each day. It is the tallest twin spired (515ft) church in the world.

Work started in 1248 and was not finally completed until 1880. It claims to house the relics of the three kings (the three wise men). I must admit I stared at the shrine and wondered could they really be there. When opened up and examined in 1864 it revealed bones and garments. I stood thoughtfully in front of the three wise men but was definitely none the wiser.

Canterbury

Our good friends Pam and Rick had moved from Holmes Chapel, where we had met, to live in Kent. We visited them and together we explored the area. One of the highlights was Canterbury Cathedral.

What an impressive cathedral it is, surrounded by lots of interesting buildings being part of another World Heritage site

(1988). The grounds include the "Old Palace" often referred to as the Archbishop's Palace where the Archbishop of Canterbury resides.

The current cathedral dates back to 1070. There was an earlier building dating back to the 6th century which was destroyed by fire in 1067. It is the home of the leader of the Church of England the Archbishop of Canterbury. He has certainly done his bit to stem the reduction in church attendance by fathering six children.

My main memory of our visit was listening to the choir practising. It was so moving I felt a tingling sensation running the length of my spine. A bit like watching the Villa beat Liverpool 7-2 (2020) only even better.

Winchester

This was one of the annual meeting of old friends John Lavender, Gary Durant and Terry Twinberrow from our Brummie youth. I think it was John who recommended Winchester and it turned out to be a good choice. The city is full of historic buildings of interest, many dating back to when it was the original capital city of England.

The cathedral is one of the largest in Europe. Building commenced in 1079. It is known by many people from the hit single "Winchester Cathedral" recorded by the New Vaudeville Band in 1966. It reached the UK top 10 and number 1 in the USA. We had seen them perform in Skegness in 1974. We knew how to have a good time!

Jane Austen died in the city in 1817 and is buried there but my lasting memory of the cathedral is a diver's helmet on a plinth at the far end. It belonged to the diver William Walker who repaired the waterlogged end of the building that was slowly sinking. He spent 6 hours a day for 6 years in dark waters packing concrete and bricks in the waterlogged area beneath the cathedral. It is reported that he saved the building from collapsing and was awarded the MVO (Member of the Victoria Order) for his service to the monarch.

The admission charge was quite high but well worth it as our guide was excellent.

Chester

Another lads trip, primarily to catch up with another friend from our young days, Brian Harris. We all grew up together but had not seen Brian for a number of years. He suggested we come and see him as he was ill and thought time was not on his side. Unfortunately, he was right. We made the trip in 2018 and 18 months later he lost his battle and was gone, but certainly not forgotten.

I thought I knew the city pretty well as I had often visited the Leeds Permanent Building Society branch when I covered the area from 1986 to 1991. We were high up walking along the city walls when we saw a sign for the cathedral, and we went down the steps to find the entrance.

Dating back to 1092 when built as an abbey, some of the Norman style can still be seen today. You can also see the remains of the Roman barracks in the Dean's field. They have an interesting way of raising money that I was happy to join. They have a huge LEGO model of the cathedral which is being built on an almost daily basis. You can buy a brick at a pound each. Over 300,000 have been sold to date. A very clever and effective money raising idea removing the need for an admission charge.

Lincoln

My late brother Steve and his wife Ann lived in the village of Boothby Graffoe just 7 miles south of the city of Lincoln. As a family we visited the cathedral in the early 1990's.

It is an impressive building and was at one time considered to be the tallest building in the world until the central spire collapsed in 1548. It was not rebuilt. It is now the fourth largest cathedral in England. For hundreds of years it housed one of the four original copies of the Magna Carta. This is now on display in the nearby Lincoln castle. During the Second World War it was safe from German bombing as it was out on loan in the United States.

The maintenance costs are a staggering £1.6 million per year. It was used in the filming of the Da Vinci Code where it was meant to be Westminster Abbey.
I hope they secured a large fee.

York

Much closer to home is England's third largest cathedral, York Minster. We have lived in Wetherby since 1991 and York is only 14 miles away. Our first visit to the city and its cathedral was in 1980 when Sue and I spent a few days of our holiday combined with collecting my new company car from Leeds.

We were living in Lichfield with baby Stephen just 7 months old when a serious fire broke out at the Minster on the 9th July 1984. It suffered major damage and took over four years and £2.25 million to repair the damage. A further £23 million was spent on major renovation work from 2007.

It is a remarkably impressive building from both the inside and out. It certainly adds to the historic feeling around that side of York. The admission fee is high at £11.50 (2020) but it is worth it especially on your first visit. Like all these old buildings maintenance costs are high and they need all the help they can get. Perhaps they could go down the LEGO route?

Lichfield

We spent two years in Lichfield when I was the Leeds PBS manager of the nearby Cannock branch (1981-83). It is one of those strange things that I saw it often, have walked around the grounds several times, but have no recollection of actually stepping inside it. Perhaps it was a case of familiarity breeding contempt. It certainly looked impressive as I walked past it on a sponsored charity walk with our good friends and neighbours Andy and Terri Bates.

In 1085 work began on replacing the wooden church with the Norman structure. This was then replaced by the current Gothic cathedral commencing in 1195. It is a real regret that I didn't make the effort to view what I am sure is an impressive interior.

Coventry

My visit was in the summer of 1964 at the age of ten. It was a school trip, and my memory of the event is a little faded. I have only been to Coventry a couple times since my first visit. Twice to watch both Villa and Blues play at the now abandoned Highfield Road stadium and also to visit my Mom's biological sister Pauline (They have a common mother and were adopted). I can remember more about the old bombed out remains of the old cathedral next door to the new one. It was a victim of a massive German bombing raid in 1941.

When we visited the cathedral, it had only been open for just two years. Designed by the architect Basil Spence it took 6 years to build which is rapid compared to medieval structures but nowhere near as impressive. It has been a useful comparison with the tradition cathedrals. I would go for the old ones every time.

On the same day we visited Kenilworth castle which I found far more interesting.

Worcester

Like Lichfield I have looked at this lovely cathedral many times, mostly sat on the boundary of the Worcester cricket club situated on the opposite bank of the River Severn. The cathedral appeared on the £20 note issued from 1999 to 2007.

Worcester has always been prone to flooding by a rising River Severn. The cathedral has a water gate that records the dates of high floods dating back as far as 1672. The last flood mark was added in the floods of 2014 when Worcester was cut in half. The cricket ground has suffered on many occasions with fixtures being forced to find a new venue often at Kidderminster CC.

A fine building of Norman/Gothic origin dating back to 1084, known for its Norman crypt and unique chapter house. Must go inside the next time I go to the cricket with my old friends from Brum.

Blue Mosque, Istanbul

Not exactly a cathedral but an important religious building in an interesting city. There are 3000 mosques in the city where East meets West. The Blue Mosque was constructed at the beginning of the 17th century. The interior is covered in hand painted blue tiles and at night the domes and minarets are bathed in blue light. I was travelling Turkey with my oldest friend John Lavender and we both found it interesting but give me a good old English gothic cathedral every time.

Sheik Zayed Grand Mosque, Abu Dhabi

I had been out to visit our friends Pam and Rick four times while they worked and lived in Abu Dhabi and then Dubai. It was on my last visit that I made it to this huge mosque, the largest in the country.

It opened in 2007 and cost a staggering $545 million. The square can hold over 40.000 worshipers. We had a very good guide who was keen to answer any questions. I must admit I stood looking across the square trying to imagine what it would be like with 40,000 people chanting. Amazing.

All of these buildings are important links with the past and how we lived. They need to treasured and maintained, whatever the cost.

7. PROMINENT PEOPLE

"In the future everyone will be famous for fifteen minutes".

Andy Warhol

"All work and no play makes Jack a dull boy"

Author James Fenimore Cooper

The one thing these people have in common is that I met them through work.

Doctor Who meets Howard from the Halifax

On a cold February night in 2001 I had just attended and enjoyed the first night of Northern Ballet's "Doctor Jekyll and Mr Hyde" sponsored by the Halifax. I came out of Sadler's Wells theatre and was relieved to see just four people in the queue for a taxi.

I immediately recognised Howard Brown, the man who promoted the Halifax current account on TV. He had obviously had a few "sherbets" at the free bar funded by the Halifax as sponsors of Northern Ballet. His partner seemed a little embarrassed by Howard's giggling. To my left a chap suddenly recognised Howard too. My goodness it was Sylvester McCoy the actor well known for his role as a rather flamboyant version of Doctor Who.

Within minutes McCoy was congratulating Howard on his TV performance and predicted further success. I found myself pointing out how well the adverts had promoted sales. Howard just smiled as his partner thanked the "Doctor" for his prognosis!

There were two guys selected in 2000 from a large number of Halifax staff to appear in our adverts. In addition to Howard from the Sheldon branch in Birmingham, there was Matt who worked in Head Office in the mortgage team which was part of my remit. Our advertising agents suggested that the first adverts (using the "Sex Bomb" tune) should feature Matt but CEO James Crosby wanted Howard to feature although I am not really sure why. James' decision proved be the right one as Howard starred in a number of well received adverts. He became a successful ambassador and the face of the Halifax before leaving in 2011.

Prior to finding success as the 7th Doctor Who, Sylvester McCoy started out as a stunt man with a reputation for putting ferrets down his trousers and even setting his head on fire. He was born Percy Kent-Smith but changed his name when he became an actor. We appear to share the questionable talent of playing the SPOONS, although I can only play after a few "sherbets". He was very pleasant and polite that evening with an absence of both ferrets and flames.

Dermot Murnaghan, TV presenter

After retiring due to my sight problems in 2002 I was fortunate to stay on the board of the HBOS Foundation. The annual award dinners were great fun. My main duty was to host a table of staff who had been invited due to their outstanding contribution in raising funds for charity.

At one dinner I did my usual thing of walking around the table welcoming the staff and thanking them for their contribution. When I reached a smartly dressed man in his mid-40's I stopped and asked, "have we met before"? "We may have done" he replied, "I am Dermot Murnaghan". With a scarlet glow I quickly apologised and scuttled back to my seat. He was a guest speaker who just happened to be on the same table.

He could have said "have I got news for you" as he has read the news for the BBC, Sky, ITV and Ch4. Known also for presenting BBC Breakfast and the quiz show EGGHEADS. He too has had embarrassing moments such as when he dropped the surname of Estonian President Toomas Hendrik ILVES and repeatedly called him President Toomas Hendrik. The president stormed off set in disgust whilst on air, shouting "he can't even get my name right".

Una Stubbs, actress

Before being taken over by the Halifax the Leeds Permanent Building Society sponsored a function room at the West Yorkshire Playhouse in Leeds. One Christmas, CEO Mike Blackburn invited families to watch Peter Pan. I was delighted to take Sue and our three children Stephen, Jenna and Claire to enjoy the show. It was so enjoyable the time flew along with some of the lost boys. Afterwards we were invited to refreshments in the "Leeds PBS" room. We were joined by members of the cast and were thrilled to be sat with Una Stubbs. She was so friendly and very good with our kids who were about 11 or 12 at the time.

Una Stubbs made her breakthrough in the hit Cliff Richard film "Summer Holiday". She auditioned as a dancer but was handed the role of Sandy. Her breakthrough into television came with the part of Rita in "Till Death Us Do Part". She went on to play many different roles including Aunt Sally in Worzel Gummidge and Mrs Hudson in "Sherlock".

Before her acting days she was the "Rowntrees chocolate girl" featuring on their Dairy Box chocolates. Although she was unaware at the time, she later discovered that her grandfather had worked at the Rowntree factory in York.

Smarties and Kit Kats were always my favourites. As far as I was concerned you could "forget the fruit gums mum".

William Hague, politician

I was invited to a dinner for the representatives of Yorkshire businesses held in Richmond North Yorkshire. I wasn't expecting much, just a nice meal with a couple of business contacts. I found myself standing in a small group indulging in the usual small talk when the double doors opened and the main guest and speaker, opposition leader William Hague was swept in by his minders. He carried on walking towards our group and came straight up to me. "Good evening, I am William Hague, delighted to meet you". I was stunned into uncharacteristic silence. Desperately struggling for a reply, I shook his outstretched hand and mumbled, "good evening". It wasn't my best conversation starter and he quickly headed off to greet other more interesting guests. I am quite lucky when it comes to winning raffles but to be the one out of probably a couple of hundred he should march right up to was a bit of a shock.

Hague was leader of the Conservative party from 1997 to 2001 and stayed an MP for Richmond until 2015. He has written several books including biographies of PM William Pitt the Younger and William Wilberforce the anti-slave campaigner. He met his wife Ffion when she was sent to teach him Welsh while he was secretary of state for Wales. They now live in a country house in Wales.

It was certainly a brief encounter but has stuck in my memory for over 20 years.

Sue Johnston, actress

Ok I'll admit it I used to watch the Ch4 soap Brookside in the 1980's in which she played one of the main characters, Sheila Grant. In 1996 the Halifax Building Society sponsored the Leeds Film Festival and Sue and I were invited to the premiere of "Brassed Off" in which the actress played the part of Vera. We were shown to our seats and I found myself sitting next to Ms Johnston. I think the extent of our conversation was an exchange of "hello's". I don't remember seeing Pete Postlethwaite or Ewan McGregor. It was however an enjoyable evening and a pleasant film.

Sue Johnston has appeared in many TV shows including Waking the Dead, Coronation Street, Downton Abbey and notably as Barbara in the Royle Family. In Brookside she played the part of Sheila the wife of Bobby Grant (played by

Ricky Tomlinson) for eight years. Later she played Tomlinson's wife in the Royle Family (1998 to 2006). She was therefore "married" to Tomlinson for 15 years which is twice as long as the total of her two actual marriages of three and four years.

Alan Hanson, footballer and presenter

As a football fan I was quite excited to attend a dinner organised by the Halifax where the former Liverpool and Scotland defender and Match of the Day pundit Alan Hanson was the after-dinner speaker. Although he was already well known as a football pundit, I was looking forward to seeing how well he would perform on his own. I was not disappointed as he delivered his well-prepared routine with enthusiasm and humour. He stayed on afterwards and when most people had left, I had a good chat with him. I was surprised how shy he was when chatting one to one. I suppose the absence of a well-prepared script made things a little more challenging. He was interesting and good company.

He was well known for his critical remarks on Match of the Day. The one that stands out is "you never win anything with kids". This often-repeated phrase was made on the opening day of the 1995/96 season. It was aimed at Man Utd who, having introduced young players including David Beckham, Paul Scholes, Nicky Butt and Gary Neville, had lost 3-1 to my team Aston Villa. United went to win both the league and FA Cup.

He got into a bit of trouble when commentating during the 1994 World Cup. He said that a player "deserves shooting" for his performance. It came the day after a Columbian defender had been shot dead after scoring an own goal.

In an interview in 2017 Hanson admitted that he had always suffered from nerves on MOTD but they got worse towards the end and were part of the reason he left.

Brian Close, cricketer

In October 1999 Yorkshire County Cricket club hosted a gala dinner to celebrate 150 years of Roses matches (Yorkshire v Lancashire). I was the guest of a Leeds solicitor who I had been working with on a joint venture with a French bank. It was obvious that he was well connected with the great and the good and insisted on introducing me to people who had little or no interest in the views of Paul Duffin. I was however delighted to shake hands and chat to a cricketing hero, Brian Close. He tried his best to look interested but seemed to be more focused on his cigarette.

He was the youngest player to be selected to play for England at the age of 18. He captained England seven times winning six and drawing one. He played his last test at the age of 45, being battered by a hostile West Indies attack. He was often a controversial figure but dedicated to the development of cricket. He was also a talented golfer who had a single figure handicap whether playing right or left-handed. It was an honour to have met him. He was now a good age but was pleasant during our brief meeting.

At the dinner there were many other old stars including Fred Trueman, and the Sky presenter, after dinner speaker and former England captain David (Bumble) Lloyd who gave a very amusing speech.

Kevin McNally, actor

Kevin has been in many TV and radio programmes, theatre productions but is probably best known for playing Joshamee Gibbs in all of the Pirates of the Caribbean movies. He was two years below me at Central School for boys but we came together in the school production of Pirates of Penzance. We were both pirates. In his case once a pirate always a pirate.

I met up with him at the Olivier Awards in 1997. Sue and I were guests of the sponsors. We were given a list of all the guests and I found Kevin's name and table number amongst a whole host of actors, producers, song writers and others from the industry. He was sat with his wife Phyllis Logan (Lady Jane in Lovejoy and Mrs Hughes in Downton Abbey).

On the table to one side of ours was the producer Trevor Nunn and his wife the actress Imogen Stubbs. On another nearby table was Robert Lindsay (My Family). There were lots of well-known people and our table was in a great position to scan for celebrities.

When the meal and awards finished, I set off and found Kevin's table. I introduced myself and reminded him that we were pirates together at school almost 30 years ago. He immediately stood up, put his arm around me and we marched off singing 'with cat like tread' from the Pirates of Penzance. I don't know if he actually remembered me, but we were both a little under the influence. He was a really good sport. I am not sure what Phyllis thought of this but I was really delighted.

He is a true all-round actor and has recently played Captain Mainwaring in a new version of Dad's Army and before that played Tony Hancock both on TV and radio. Back in the 80' he co-wrote episodes of Minder and Boon. A really talented chap.

There were one or two other well-known people who also went to Central Grammar school including the actor Nicol Williamson, John Lodge of the Moody Blues and Bob Carolgees of TISWAS fame but unfortunately without Spit the dog.

Most of these meetings were very brief but memorable.

8. THE FAB FOUR AND ME

"My model for business is the Beatles. They were four guys who kept each other's' negative tendencies in check, they balanced each other. And the total was greater than the sum of the parts"

Steve Jobs (former Apple CEO)

My first memory of the Beatles was at the Hobmoor Road Primary school's Christmas party in December 1963. I have no idea who brought the Beatles single "She Loves You" to the party but from that day forward, at the age of ten, I was a Beatles fan.

First single bought

Just three months later in March 1964 they released "Can't Buy Me Love" and despite having nothing to play it on I bought it from Woolworth's at the Yew Tree. You could accuse me of blackmailing my dad into buying a record player. Fortunately, he loved music and immediately bought a rather well used and very basic player from a work colleague. My brother Steve and I were delighted and very grateful. Steve bought the Animals "Baby let me take you home" and dad went out and bought the soundtrack of South Pacific. Everyone was happy. Mum had to wait for Ken Dodd's "Tears".

"Can't Buy Me Love" went straight to number one. The B side was "You Can't Do That" which I still think is a great track. Interesting to know that Paul McCartney wrote the A side and John Lennon the B side. They put all their songs under the Lennon and McCartney brand irrespective of who was the main writer. Some were written almost alone. Some joint but all were eventually brought together for final agreement.

The A side was written and recorded in Paris while the group were appearing in the French capital. My grandad was surprised by my love of the new group and told me in a good humoured fashion that they wouldn't last for long. He then opened his diary and put a note in for the last day of December 1964 "The Beatles still around"? He was good enough to admit defeat at the end of the year.

My first EP

I decided to catch up with some of the Beatles songs I had missed. I walked up Church Road to the record shop just past the model shop. I bought the "Beatles Hits" EP (extended player) which had four good tracks.

It included their first single "Love Me Do' released on 5th October 1962 and reached No 17 in the UK charts. There were two versions recorded with Ringo on drums for one and a session drummer on the other. The main composer was Paul.

"Please Please Me" was released on 11th January 1963. It reached number 2 in the UK. This was the track that made the music industry sit up and take notice of the Fab Four. Main composer John.

"From Me to You" was their first number 1 after its release on 11th April 1963. A truly joint composition written whilst on tour with a very young Helen Shapiro.

"Thank You Girl" was the weakest track on the EP which is hardly surprising as it was the B side of "From Me to You".

I was really pleased with my purchase and played it until I knew every word. I would then dance around the house singing and driving the rest of the family mad.

My first album

Their first two albums (LP's, Long Players) were "Please Please Me" and "With the Beatles". These early albums both featured tracks written by Paul and John plus covers of other artists songs, such as "A Taste of Honey".

In July 1964 the Beatles film "A Hard Day's Night" was released. I was very excited when my dad announced we would all be off to the pictures to see it. We all enjoyed it which led to me putting the soundtrack album top of my Christmas list. It duly arrived and was played and played. It is my favourite all time album as it was such an early influence.

It still amuses me to see old Albert Steptoe (Wilfred Brambell) playing the part of Paul's grandad in the film. There are some great tracks, all written by Lennon and McCartney. Interestingly the eight tracks they wrote on their first album were credited to McCartney and Lennon, but this had now changed to Lennon and McCartney. Seven of the 13 tracks were from the film. "I'll Cry Instead" was written for the film but was cut at the last moment.

The film was a great success as was the album. Almost exactly a year later their next film "Help" was released as was the soundtrack album. Off we went again as a family to see it. Guess what? Yes, you are right, it was top of my 1965 Christmas list. Unlike previous albums two tracks were written and credited to George and Ringo was given "Act Naturally" to perform.

The Beatles were starting to lead changes in the pop world. This album introduced the use of other instruments, including flutes, and the use of 4 track recording. Paul sang "Yesterday" on his own. Times they were a changing.

Influencing the world

I was only 10 when the Beatles arrived in America in February 1964. They took the nation by storm. It had taken them a few years to establish themselves in the UK, but America was taken almost overnight. By April 1964 they had all the top 5 selling singles in the Billboard chart. Remarkable.

When they appeared on the Ed Sullivan show the audience of 73 million was the second highest ever. The highest being when JFK was assassinated 11 weeks earlier.

The impact was amazing. The mop top hairstyles were copied as boys wanted to be a Beatle and girls wanted to grab hold of them. Parents were dismayed or furious.

Many young boys were keen to pick up a guitar. Bruce Springsteen and Tom Petty both claim that it was the Beatles' arrival that made them first strum. One of the guests on the same Ed Sullivan show was 17 year old Brit Davy Jones who was appearing on Broadway in "Oliver" with Tessie O'Shea. He was spellbound by the group and said he wanted to be like them. A year later he was one of the Monkees, a group put together to take part in an American TV show about a group just like the Beatles. The Monkees were very successful, selling 75 million records. They didn't just monkey around. I watched their TV sitcom and liked some of their records but never bought any.

A long pause

I think mainly due to the absence of cash I didn't buy another Beatles album until the "White album" and even then it was slightly second hand, bought from a friend. It was a real mixed bag double album that arguably should have been cut down to one.

"Sgt Pepper" (1967) was a huge development. Their touring had ended, and they spent three months preparing and it shows. They spent hours perfecting each song, unlike their first album which took only one day to record.

It started out as Paul's idea for a themed album but that tailed off as tracks were developed. There are no real gaps between each track and the inclusion of George's "Within you, without you" adds a new dimension.

It had other new features such as including the lyrics one the "book like" fold doubling the cover. Inside the other cover was a sheet of "goodies" to play with. These included a cardboard moustache and military stripes. It showed such invention that it is now regarded as their best work. I bought the CD later but missed out on the goodies.

Although I paused from buying their albums after "Help" and the "White album" until the arrival of Compact Discs and spare cash, I continued buying their singles until they split in 1971.

Singles that bring back memories

Some Beatles songs just launch my mind back to certain events.

Dad fell ill in November 1964. Steve and I clubbed together and bought him "I Feel Fine" to cheer him up. I am sure that wasn't the only reason. As always, he took it well and smiled as we gave it to him on his 44th birthday. Not long after in May 1966 I bought "Paperback Writer" little knowing that 50 years later I would publish my first one.

In my second year at Central GS a French student teacher arrived and took some of our lessons. Near the end of the school year the Beatles launched "All You Need Is Love". It starts with part of the French National Anthem. With the long summer holiday about to start we could not resist welcoming him to the lesson with our best attempts to recapture the beginning of the hit single. He was not amused.

Their single "Hello Goodbye" was the Christmas number one in December 1967. Ever since then I have always felt the Christmas spirit as soon as I hear the opening "You say yes, I say no". John fought hard for his "I am a Walrus" to be the A side but it lost to Paul's more commercial song.

With their other halves (WAGS)

The first Beatle to get married was John in 1962. "Well, we will just have to get married then" he was heard to say when Cynthia announced she was pregnant with Julian.

Their marriage lasted until the arrival of Yoko Ono whom he married in 1969. John took a couple years off from Yoko in 1973 with May Pang. He came back to Yoko in 1975 with pangs of regret and stayed until he was shot and tragically died in 1980 aged just 40.

John was a talented force. He certainly worked well with the other members of the band particularly Paul. There was always a little something out of the ordinary with him though. I remember thinking how daft he was lying in bed with Yoko in the Amsterdam Hilton. Did he really think lying in bed would make a scrap of difference to world peace or was it just to help promote his new Plastic Ono Band?

Next up was Ringo who married hairdresser Maureen in 1963. They had three children. The eldest Zak has followed his dad and has been the drummer for a number of bands including Oasis but the most notable has been The Who. He started with them in 1996 and is still with them. He has also played with his dad on many occasions.

Ringo met the Bond actress Barbara Bach on a film set in 1980 and they were married a year later. They seem happy enough as Ringo enters his 80's.

Always Mr Nice guy and acting naturally, he was the least talented member, but you can't help liking the guy.

Third up was George who married the model Pattie Boyd in 1966. They tried unsuccessfully to have a family and George refused to consider adoption. Boyd eventually walked out after George allegedly had a fling with Ringo's ex-wife Maureen. They divorced amicably in 1977. A year later, George married Olivia Arias who worked in the record industry. Pattie married George's good friend guitarist Eric Clapton in 1979. George's son Dhani Harrison was 22 when George died from cancer and has continued in the music business.

I always liked George. He produced some great music as a solo artist, and I loved the Travelling Wilburys music. "Handle with Care" was their standout track for me.

Last to fully commit was Paul. He came close to marrying the actress Jane Asher. They announced their engagement on Christmas Day 1967, but Paul was caught offside when Jane returned early to their home from a trip and it was all over after 5 years.

It wasn't long before Paul fell for the photographer Linda Eastman and they married in 1969. Linda already had a daughter Heather from a previous marriage. Heather was soon adopted by Paul. Linda was brought into Paul's band Wings where she played keyboard. She was not a very proficient player. Rather unfairly she received some nasty criticism. They had three children together. James has followed his dad into the music industry. Stella is a very successful fashion designer and Mary is a successful photographer. Sadly, Linda died of breast cancer at the age of 56 in 1998.

Paul's next union was a bit of a surprise when he married Heather Mills in 2002. I saw her dancing in front of Paul's band in Sheffield. The marriage didn't last, and they divorced in 2008. He now appears very happy and settled with Nancy (Shewell) whom he married in 2011.

He was always my favourite and am lucky to have seen him perform in both Sheffield and Abu Dhabi. He always seemed to have a good approach to dealing with the media and the public. Extremely talented composer and a pretty good bass player. Could have taught John to smile and relax a bit more.

Things I did not know

Before they broke into the big time John went on a two-week holiday to Spain with Manager Brian Epstein. Brian was known to be gay and there were lots of rumours at the time. John was known to be keen to experiment in all sorts of ways.

Tongues wagged and John denied all the accusations. So much so that allegedly he put one of his friends in hospital at Paul's 21st party when jokes about the trip were made in his direction.

Of all the Beatles John came from the most relatively well-off family. On his 21st birthday his Aunt Margaret gave him £100 (worth about £2000 today). John took Paul for few days holiday in Paris. They had their hair cut in a style suggested by a French friend and the "Mop Tops" were crowned.

"She's leaving home" was a track on the Sgt Pepper album. Paul wrote the melody and words after reading a newspaper article about the disappearance of Melanie Coe aged 17. What Paul didn't know when writing it was that he had met Melanie three years earlier when he judged her the winner of a dance competition on Ready Steady Go. In real life Melanie Coe was found and returned to her parents. Great track and good story.

The Beatles were a great band that changed many things and influenced a lot of people. They certainly made me really enjoy music.

Yosemite with Steve

Sydney

Sydney from the helicopter

China standing up….and lying down (see Chapter 2)

Egypt

Egypt

9. BANDS ON THE RUN

"Music touches us emotionally, where words alone can't".

Actor Johnny Depp

I still can't believe I saw 40 live bands while I was still at school. No wonder my 'O' Levels didn't go well first-time round! Perhaps if there had been an 'O' level or two on Prog (progressive) rock I might have done better.

Derek and the Dominos featuring Eric Clapton

I managed to get to the famous Birmingham music venue "Mothers" found above a furniture store in Erdington Birmingham on just three occasions before it closed in January 1971. I was lucky that one of these was to see Derek and the Dominos featuring Eric Clapton. The room was dangerously overcrowded with people coming up through the fire escape and blocking the main stairs. It was so hot that the band kept leaving the stage to recover. My friend Brian Harris and I left before the end because we had to catch the last number 11 bus back to the Yew Tree. We had school the next day.

Clapton started out with the Yardbirds and found further fame with Cream and Blind Faith. He became a friend of Beatle George Harrison and played lead guitar on the Beatles "While My Guitar Gently Weeps" which was written by Harrison. The single "Badge" that appeared on the last Cream album "Goodbye" was written by Clapton and Harrison.

It is great to say I saw Clapton in 1970 but the night was spoilt somewhat by the overcrowding and early exit.

The Who

Another interesting music venue in the early 70's was the Mayfair Suite situated in the Bull Ring. When bands were playing it branded itself as "Kinetic Circus". It was a large room designed for many purposes not just music and the acoustics suffered as a result.

The first band I saw there was The Who on 12th May 1971. The lights went down and loud music came through the enormous speakers but the band members were not to be seen just yet. After a couple of minutes, they came on stage and began to play live as the backing track ended. It was "Won't Get Fooled Again". It wasn't released, as a much shorter single, for another 6 weeks and the extended album version for another 3 months. The impact was electrifying, and it was an unforgettable experience. Drummer Keith Moon bashed away like only "Moon the loon" could. A great night.

Lead guitarist Pete Townsend is well known for smashing up his guitars on stage. I can't remember if he did that night. There is no accurate record of how many he has destroyed but according to an analysis by "thewhonet" he got through 37 in 1967 alone!

Led Zeppelin

Zeppelin were at the top of their game when we saw them at Kinetic Circus in November '71. Boy they were loud. It was a bit of a relief when the strains of "Stairway to Heaven" were heard. The album Led Zeppelin IV featuring Stairway to Heaven was released just 2 days before we saw them. Apart from loud they were long. Their set was almost 3 hours and contained all their most loved numbers including "Black Dog" and of course "Whole lotta Love". I kept my ticket stub until a few years ago when Gary Durant sold it for me to a collector for £75.

Led Zeppelin sold over 111 million records but never released any singles in the UK. They were successful across the world particularly in the USA. Like the Who they also lost their drummer, John Bonham two years after Moon had been eclipsed. Both had alcohol related deaths at the age of 32 years.

The Faces, featuring Rod Stewart

We paid further visits to Kinetic Circus to see Uriah Heap, Anibus and Mountain (featuring Les West). Our last visit in October 1972 was a very good night enjoying Faces featuring Rod Stewart.

Faces were formed in 1969 but Stewart continued to develop a solo career much to the growing concern of the group. On the night he sang some of his hits including Maggie May. When I started work in September 1971, I went on day release to Matthew Boulton College. Between the afternoon and evening lectures we went to a café called "The Tow Rope" whose juke box regularly blasted out Maggie May. Every time I heard it I started to feel hungry whatever time of day or night.

In his youth Rod was a keen footballer and had a trial with Brentford. It was unsuccessful and he was never called back. In 1969 he recorded guest vocals for the Australian Python Lee Jackson song "In a Broken Dream". It was not released until the next year. His payment for a song that was a success when re-released in 1972 was a set of car seat covers. Definitely a new cover version.

Elton John

I received Elton John's second album "Elton John" as a 1970 Christmas present and played it until the grooves almost disappeared. "Your Song" is probably the only song that I know all the words to. Something not all those who have heard me reproduce it seem to fully appreciate. He was almost the last act to perform at "Mothers" before it closed in January 1971.

I was keen to see him perform after missing the Mothers date and came close to seeing him perform at the end of 1971 when he was playing at the Town Hall in the centre of Birmingham. The other lads went but I didn't because I had a better offer. Or I thought I did. It was my first date with Glynis Coles and I took her to the White Hart pub on Tile Cross

Road. The next night we went to the recording of the TV show "Braden's Week" at Pebble Mill where Esther Rantzen turned and offered us a chip during the section on Birmingham chip shops. We were seen by many people. The next night I was dumped by a "Dear John" letter. Actually, it did say dear Paul. Mind you she was very attractive and the lad she had fallen out with the previous week had a set of wheels. I only had a bus pass.

I had to wait another 20 years until I finally caught up with Elton at Wembley. Sue and I went courtesy of The Bank of Scotland who processed our credit cards. It was worth the wait. Billy Joel should have been there too but was ill so Elton doubled his set and included some of Billy Joel's songs.

Somewhat surprisingly Elton John is Sean Lennon's godfather. John Lennon's last public performance was singing three songs with Elton at his concert at Madison Square Gardens in 1975. Elton's surname name, John, which replaced Dwight came from Long JOHN Baldry.

Fleetwood Mac

The composition of the band has changed a lot since it was formed back in 1967. Two of the original members were responsible for the name; Mick *FLEETWOO*D and John *Mc (MAC)Vie*. They are both still key members. I have been lucky to see a more recent line up on two occasions in 2003 and 2009. On both occasions it was Mick Fleetwood, John McVie, Stevie Nicks and Lindsey Buckingham. Chrissie McVie (previously known as Christine Perfect) was there when they recorded "Rumours" but dropped out for a few years partly due to her fear of flying. She is now back with them.

Fleetwood Mac have sold over 120 million records including over 40 million of the album Rumours alone. During the recording of Rumours the band members were under extreme emotional and business pressure not helped by an oversupply of drugs and alcohol. Nicks and Buckingham's relationship ended. Nicks and Fleetwood had a brief pairing. It was chaos, but amazingly the album was positively affected. One track from the album had a very successful formula. Every member of the group contributed to "The Chain" and it became the theme tune for BBC and Ch4 coverage of Formula 1 motor racing.

Stevie Nicks went on to have a relationship with two of the Eagles; Don Henley and Joe Walsh. Mick Fleetwood has made some acting appearances including a guest role in Star Trek.

A great band that has survived a huge number of changes.

David Bowie

I am not too sure why I went to see Bowie with my friends Gary Durant and Brian Harris at Birmingham Town Hall in March 1972. It was probably Brian's idea as he was a big influence on our choice of music. Bowie had brought out the "Hunky Dory" album a few months before, which Brian had bought. What was surprising about the gig was that the Town Hall was only about half full with no one in the first floor seats. The other memorable thing was the profusion of leaflets promoting his new single "Starman" which came out a couple of weeks later in April '72.

Bowie was born David Jones but changed his name to avoid being confused with Davy Jones from the American response to the Beatles, the Monkees. He pronounced his new surname like you say Joey. He was at school with Pete Frampton (a member of Humble Pie) and also knew Elton John when he was young and called Reg Dwight.

Bowie had an early single release in 1967. "The Laughing Gnome" was a novelty record and did not chart but it did come back to haunt him. In 1990 Bowie announced he would launch a telephone vote to decide the songs to be played on his greatest hits "Sound and Vision" tour. The New Musical Express went all out to try to get the Laughing Gnome listed with a "just say Gnome "campaign. Not surprisingly Bowie scrapped the vote and didn't play the song on tour. Not even on the UK section when he was Gnome from Gnome!

He was married twice but had said at one point he was bisexual. In later life he was the voice of Lord Royal Highway in the cartoon SpongeBob SquarePants.

A talented singer, song writer and actor Bowie was a success in both music and films, selling over 100 million records and appearing in over 30 films. His son from his first marriage, Duncan Jones (originally called Zowie), is a successful film producer.

Emerson Lake and Palmer

I always referred to them as ELP. I saw them twice, both times at the Odeon New Street in Birmingham. The first time was at the end of 1971, then a year later at the end of '72. I recorded in my diary that they were "brilliant". Keith Emerson was a very talented keyboard player if a little eccentric as he was prone to stabbing his keyboard when the knives came out. They sold over 48 million albums as they rose to fame following a great performance at the Isle of Wight Festival in 1970. All three members had great pedigrees. Keith Emerson had played in The Nice. Guitarist Greg Lake in King Crimson and drummer Carl Palmer in Atomic Rooster.

Their music went from long raucous keyboard dominated heavy rock (eg Tarkus) to acoustic (Take a pebble). They also crossed into classical music with the album "Pictures at an Exhibition" which they launched at a huge discount. I bought this and the albums Emerson Lake and Palmer (1970) and Tarkus (1971) which also appeared in my record collection

Carl Palmer was born in Handsworth Birmingham a couple of streets from where my brother and I were born and only three weeks after my brother's birth. Carl's brother was a drummer with Canyon, a Birmingham band we saw a few times at the Bulls Head near the Swan in Yardley.

Sadly, Emerson suffered with depression in later life and died when he shot himself in the head in 2016. Later the same year Greg Lake passed away with cancer.

A full list of all the acts I have seen can be found in the appendix at the end of this book.

10. MUSICALS ENJOYED

"Maybe I am old fashioned. But I remember the beauty and thrill of being moved by musicals. Particularly the endings of shows"
Composer, Marvin Hamlisch

I have been very fortunate to see the performance of many top-class musicals. (see appendix for the full list) It is one of the cruellest effects of losing most of my sight and hearing that I will never be able to enjoy another.

Hair

This was my first musical way back on the 24th April 1971 (cost 50p). Yes, I still have the programme and ticket stub. I was 17 still at school and just about to resit my O Levels.

I went with my good friends to this day John Lavender and Gary Durant. The highlight of the evening was when we were invited to leap on to the stage and dance with the cast in the finale "Be in". I was up there like a shot definitely wanting to "be in" not out. I danced with a rather attractive young lady but sadly not for long enough. She would soon "be off" and so were we.

It was a large cast, and I can see from the programme that the only cast member to be remembered was Joan Armatrading who had a very small part as a member of the "tribe".
She probably had a lot of support in the audience, having grown up in Birmingham from the age of 3. The following year she released her first album "Whatever's for us". She went on to win the Ivor Novello award for contemporary Song Collection in 1996. Outside of her music Joan completed a History degree from the Open University.

Aspects of Love

The music was written by Andrew Lloyd Webber with lyrics by Don Black and Charles Hart. It opened at the Prince of Wales theatre in 1989 starring Michael Ball. We went to see it with our good friends Pam and Rick Firth in the December. We loved it and saw it again when it came to Leeds in 2008. Our favourite tune was "Love changes everything".

Up until just 2 weeks before the first opening night, the famous James Bond actor Roger Moore was due to play the part of George. He pulled out at this late stage saying he was struggling to cope with the technical aspects of singing with an orchestra. His late decision was not the action of a saint but a great break for his understudy Kevin Colson. When he was informed, he was said to be shaken but soon stirred.

Michael Ball was excellent in the lead role of Alex in Aspects, but his first performance was as an actor rather than a singer. In 1984 he played the role of Malcolm Nuttall in Coronation Street. He now lives with his partner, former Ready Steady Go (rock/pop programme 1963 to 66) presenter Cathy McGowan. They met when he was rehearsing for Aspects in 1989.

Phantom of the Opera

Michael Crawford was the original Phantom but when we saw it he had gone to perform the show on Broadway and David Willetts had taken his place. We still enjoyed it, again with friends Pam and Rick." Phantom" was the world's most successful show taking $6 billion before it was overtaken by The Lion King. It was seen by 130 million people in 27 countries.

Crawford was born with his mother's surname, Smith. His mother's first husband had died a couple of years before and the father was not named. She then married a Mr Ingram, but he was brought up by his mother's family, the Pikes. His surname became confusing, and it was often the case that Michael was told "don't tell them your name's Pike".

He was a regular performer and came to national recognition as Frank Spencer in the comedy "Some Mothers Do 'Ave 'Em. The part was originally offered to Ronnie Barker but both Ronnie and Norman Wisdom turned it down. Difficult to imagine Ronnie Barker on roller skates.

He was awarded the part of the Phantom after Andrew Lloyd Webber heard him practising with the singing coach of Lloyd Webber's then wife Sarah Brightman. For a while the favourite to play the role was Steve Harley (the cockney rebel) but Lloyd Webber changed his mind as the songs became less rock and more operatic.

I went on to see many more Lloyd Webber shows but Aspects and Phantom remained the favourites.

The Pirates of Penzance

By the time I saw this in Leeds in 1997 it was well over 100 years since its first performance. This was no D'Oyly Carte offering as it was fun all the way. The light opera was still based on the work of Gilbert and Sullivan but presented in a far more modern and amusing context. This approach was aided considerably by the star performance of Paul Nicholas.

Nicholas was born in Peterborough and his father was a former MI6 agent. He started out as a pop singer using the name Paul Dean (even working with David Bowie). He turned to acting and was made famous by playing Vince in the TV comedy "Just Good Friends" alongside the lovely Jan Francis who became well known for playing Lisa Colbert in "Secret Army".

Like many veteran actors Paul Nicholas has appeared in a soap; EastEnders as Gavin Sullivan. He was in 30 episodes from August 2015 to July 2016. He is also a producer both professionally and privately as he has fathered 6 children with 4 different mothers, two of which were before his first marriage or reaching 21. A real producer.

Jersey Boys

This was certainly a move away from opera into the Pop world and proved a really enjoyable night out in London with our friends Barbara and Dennis Skinner. The story of the pop group The Four Seasons complete with their great hit songs is a real treat. "*Oh What a Night*" it certainly was!

Four Seasons lead singer Frankie Valli has had almost countless hits outside the group. He has also had several acting roles including two seasons (5 & 6 but not the 4th Season!) playing the mobster Rusty Millio in the brilliant "Sopranos" TV series.

Chicago

When working for the Halifax if I had an early meeting to attend in London I would travel down the night before and try to get a last-minute ticket to a West End show. In 2000 I was lucky enough to get to see Chicago. It is the story of corruption and the involvement of a celebrity criminal. Not my favourite musical but enjoyable and certainly much better than spending the evening in my hotel room.

On that night the role of Amos Hart, the husband of the murderess Roxie Hart, was played by the comedian Les Dennis.
Les made his breakthrough winning the talent show "New Faces" with a record score of 119 out of 120. It was so long ago that one of the judges was Arthur Askey (1900-1982). Les is probably best known for hosting Family Fortunes.

Some of the amusing incorrect answers from the show include:

An animal with horns ….. "a *Bee*"

Something too BIG to fit inside a mini…..*"a mouse"*

Something a train spotter would have in his pocket…… *"a magnifying glass"*

A measurement of liquid…… *"paint"*

A fast animal…..*"hippo"*

Something you might find in a garage….. *"grand piano"*

More recently he appeared in Coronation Street in 2014 as Michael Rodwell before being killed off in November 2016. A year later he played Uncle Fester whilst touring in the Addams Family.

He was once married to Amanda Holden until Neil Morrissey "Behaved Badly" with her.

Oliver

I am a fan of Charles Dickens and have read many of his books, but this is the only one I have seen on stage, albeit the Lionel Bart musical version. Fortunately, sitting just a couple of rows from the front I could just about still see and hear enough to thoroughly enjoy the spectacular performance in Leeds 2012. The dancing, singing and acting were all marvellous. We all wanted to ask for "more".

Lionel Bart's first performance of Oliver was in 1960 and there have since been 3 stage revivals. When Bart was desperate for money he sold the rights of the show to Max Bygraves for just £350. Bygraves later sold them for £250,000, but still wanted to tell the story.

Somewhat surprisingly the actor, voice artist and comedian Neil Morrissey was chosen by Cameron Mackintosh to take the part of the Jewish miser Fagin in this production. His performance was excellent. He was unrecognisable due to his clothes and make up and may still have been hiding from Les Dennis!

Morrissey spent much of his childhood in Staffordshire care homes. His two most notable professional performances were as one of the "Men Behaving Badly", and the voice of the children's cartoon character "Bob the Builder". His performance demonstrated he could also sing and dance.

We Will Rock You

Sue and I saw several pop/rock musicals.   Just nudged out of top spot by Jersey Boys was We Will Rock You. Launched in the West End in 2002 it tells the story of the legendary rock group, Queen. I have always liked their music and the show did them proud. It had a long run in the West End until 2014. I would have loved seeing their last two performances as original Queen members Roger Taylor and Brian May took part, rising through the stage floor in a blanket of smoke.

The highly accomplished guitarist Brian May still plays a very unusual guitar: the "Red Special". It was made by May and his father, an electronics engineer, when he was 16. It was made from a piece of an 18th century wooden fireplace, motor bike valve springs, shelf edging and mother of pearl buttons. May plays it using a six pence piece as a plectrum claiming it gave a better sound than the usual plastic ones.

I only saw him perform live once when Queen toured with Paul Rodgers replacing the late Freddie Mercury. This was in Birmingham with my good friend Martin Wood. I was a big fan of Free and had seen Paul Rodgers perform as their lead singer three times back in the early 70's. The new combination was excellent but still wish I had seen them with Freddie.

Whenever I hear the Queen song "Another one bites the DUST" a smile comes straight to my face. I immediately think of the diet group in "Little Britain" comedy where Matt Lucas says "the best thing to eat to ensure weight loss is "Dust".

Singing in the Rain

Of the classics we saw one really stands out for two reasons. I decided to splash out on "Singing in the Rain" as a Christmas treat for the family. This was when I had just started to experience real problems with my sight. During the performance I could only see the bottom half of everything. Naturally I was very worried. In addition, this was made worse by being just a couple of rows from the front and getting soaked in the rain that splashed from the excellent dance routines. Apart from that it was a good performance. This was Christmas 2001. A couple of weeks later I had virtually no sight in my left eye. The vision in my right had never fully developed due to a squint that was not spotted until I was 7 or 8 years old during a school medical. My hearing loss came much later.

Gene Kelly and Debbie Reynolds starred in the famous film back in 1952. It opened to a fairly quiet critical response. However, it is now regarded as one of the best film musicals. There are a couple of myths surrounding the famous Kelly street dance in the rain. There were claims that milk was added to the rain to make it stand out more on screen. Apparently, they just used very well-placed back lighting. Rumours that it is shot in a single take are also found to be incorrect as it actually took nearly 3 days to complete.

Acorn Antiques

I have only seen two musicals that could clearly be defined as comedies; The Monty Python based Spamalot and Victoria Wood's   Acorn Antiques which first saw light as part of "Victoria Wood As seen on TV" comedy sketch show.

The original sketch in 1985 featured Celia Imrie (as Miss Babs), Victoria Wood (Miss Berta), Duncan Preston (Clifford) and Julie Walters (Mrs Overall). They all returned with the launch of the musical in 2005 with Walters and Wood alternating as Mrs Overall. Neil Morrissey and Josie Lawrence (whose line is it anyway) were added as two new characters.

By the time Sue and I saw it in Leeds two years later the stars had been replaced by very talented alternatives. Overall, it was a splendid evening's entertainment.

Without any doubt Mrs Overall was my favourite character. Julie Walters is a very talented actor whatever role she adopts but I loved her Mrs O' in the TV sketches. I can't remember the last time I had a macaroon, but you can't always have your cake and eat it.

Dame Julie Walters is a Brummie, born in Edgbaston just two weeks after my late brother Steve was born a couple of miles away. She briefly trained as a nurse at the Queen Elizabeth hospital before turning to acting. She recovered from bowel cancer in 2018 and lives on an organic farm with her husband Grant Roffey in West Sussex.

A full list of musicals enjoyed can be found in the appendix at the end of the book.

11. YOU'RE HAVING A LAUGH

"I think contraception should be used on every conceivable occasion"

Spike Milligan

I have seen a few comedians perform live over the years and have rarely, if indeed ever, been disappointed.

Tommy Trinder (1909-1989)

My earliest recollection of seeing a comedian on stage was in 1962 at the Pier Theatre Eastbourne. Tommy Trinder was a popular comedian at the time. I was only 8 years old but fully understood the meaning of his rendition of *"I saw Susie sitting in a shoeshine shop" (all day long she sits and shines, all day long she shines and sits)*. I can still hear Tommy singing it bringing a smile back to my face. I am not sure my parents approved but cannot recall them commenting.

He was the original compere for Sunday Night at the London Palladium before Bruce Forsyth. The only joke he seems to be remembered for was one he made during the war in 1940. He had been walking down Whitehall when a chap pointed, looking a little lost, asked him "which side is the War Office on?" "Ours I think" replied Trinder.

He was a lifelong supporter of Fulham FC and was their chairman from 1959 to 1976.

Ken Dodd (1927-2018)

The other one I saw when I was quite young back in January 1966 was Ken Dodd. He was starring in the Humpty Dumpty pantomime at the Birmingham Hippodrome. I can only remember his tickling stick and of course the Diddy Men from Knotty Ash. I was tickled even back in the stalls and my mom loved his singing.

Doddy hit the headlines in 1989 when he was charged with tax evasion. Over
£300,000 was found stashed in 3 suitcases in his loft. When asked by the judge what it felt like to have £100,000 in a suitcase Doddy replied *"the notes are very light M'Lord"*. He was acquitted but many audiences have since had a long sentence as he was known for not leaving the stage early.

Tony Hancock (1924-1968)

Hancock was born in Southam Road, Hall Green, Birmingham in 1924. Not far from where I was brought up in Yardley. There is a plaque on the wall of the house he was born in which I have seen as I knew people who lived in the same road in the 1960's. He moved down south with his parents when he was about 3 years old. He was at his peak in the 50's but I grew to love the radio repeats of Hancock's Half Hour in my teens. In the famous Blood Donor *("a pint? that's very nearly an armful"),* he read his lines from teleprompters as he was recovering from a recent car crash. He often used the device in subsequent television recordings.

My favourite radio episodes were "Sunday afternoon at home" where they were all bored with nothing to do and "Wild man of the woods" where Kenneth Williams declared he was the "sole survivor of a tandem crash". I still use some of Hancock's phrases like when someone says, "it's raining you know" I can cheekily reply "so that's what's making the road wet".

Other famous lines: "Does Magna Carta mean nothing; did she die in vain?"
"Hypochondria is the only illness I haven't got".

Sadly, Hancock died in Australia in 1968 aged 44 when I was 14. "Stone me what a life".

Eric Sykes (1923-2012)

The funniest live show I ever saw was "Big Bad Mouse" starring Eric Sykes and Jimmy Edwards in December 1975. It was hilarious from start to finish and I rocked back and forwards with laughter. However, I am not sure my date Frankie was in quite such a helpless state. Big Bad Mouse was centred on events taking place in an office but like one you have never seen. Apart from the cleverly written script there were plenty of funny physical moments with Sykes going out of a window instead of the door. After the show had been running for about ten minutes a group of people entered the stalls and made their way across a row of seats. Sykes stopped the performance and addressed the late comers. "I suppose you want us to go back and start again from the beginning". And they did, but at an incredibly rapid pace. It was obviously something they had perfected, and it brought the house down, ending with rapturous applause.

Sykes was a prolific comedy writer (for the Goons and many others) and performer (Sykes, with Hattie Jacques). He was profoundly deaf. It started during the Second World War and despite two operations it did not improve. He wore spectacles that had hearing aids built into the arms. More recently he was a voice on the children's show Teletubbies.

Frank Skinner

Almost a Brummie as he was born in West Bromwich in 1957. Christened and known by his friends as Chris his parents called him by his middle name, Graham. He was forced to change to his stage name as there was already a singer called Chris Collins. He chose to use the name of one of his dad's domino team. You could say it was a game changer He named his son Buzz (b.2012).

In the early days he performed at the Hare and Hounds pub in Kings Heath Birmingham where I used to meet up with football teammates when I played for Waterford Celtic in the early 70's. I always found it strange that our manager insisted on meeting there on a Sunday lunch time as one or two of our team would have a couple of jars before the afternoon kick off. I was disappointed to learn that the pub is very unlikely to reopen after being closed during the 2020 pandemic.

I saw Skinner perform live at Harrogate International with my good friend Andy Bates. Frank deliberately refrained from swearing for half his show to prove that he could get as many laughs. He did. A good challenge for a practising Roman Catholic. Apart from both being born not far from each other we also have the Ukulele in common. I only got as far as the basics, being tutored by the very patient late Mel Swales. Frank is now quite a competent player. I wouldn't put my Uke in Room 101 but I might be tempted to put his football team West Bromwich Albion in there even though my mom's family were also supporters of the "baggies".

Andy Parsons

Probably best known for regularly appearing on *Mock the Week*. The comedian and writer is a keen cricket fan. I was surprised when he came on stage in Harrogate when I went to see Jonathan Agnew and Geoffrey Boycott perform a very entertaining "An evening with…". Parsons was both funny and interesting. I also saw the Cambridge Law graduate perform his stand-up comedy routine at the Edinburgh Fringe in 2009 with Sue and our friends Pam and Rick.

John Cleese

Another Cambridge law graduate. Cleese was born in Weston Super Mare in 1939. His family surname was originally Cheese until his father became so cheesed off with it, he changed it by deed poll to Cleese in 1923.

He wrote and starred in my favourite TV comedy Fawlty Towers in the 1970's. Only 12 episodes but a comedy gem.

One of his great passions has been the protection of Lemurs which he developed during work on the film "Fierce Creatures" *(1998)*. The film starred many of the cast from the successful "A Fish Called Wanda" (1988) but was not well received and did not cover even half of its production costs of $25million. A new species of lemur was discovered in 1990 and was christened "Cleese's woolly lemur".

I have seen Cleese live twice, most recently in York when he was on his "Alimony Tour"
In 2010. He was openly raising money to fund his most recent divorce. It was a little disappointing as he used old video clips for much of the show. The first time was in 1973 when the Monty Python team toured the country with their first "farewell tour". I still have the programme which cost 10p. It took them another 41 years to actually finish with more than a few "bob" in their pockets by appearing for several performances at the O2 arena in London!

Bernard Manning (1930-2007)

He was born and raised in the pre-Politically Correct (PC) world in a poor area of Manchester by parents of a mixture of Russian, Jewish and Irish ancestry.

During his national service he claimed to have guarded Rudolf Hess (Adolf Hitler's deputy) in Berlin. It was during his army days that he discovered a talent for singing, telling jokes and charging people to watch.

I saw him in Skegness in the early 70's. What else was there to do in the bracing east coast resort except perhaps for live wrestling, and we were very afraid of the vicious old ladies wielding their walking sticks. Although clearly breaching today's PC culture he did make us laugh. Particularly when he gave my good friend John Lavender a ton of abuse as he left his seat on his way to the toilet and even worse on the way back. But 'Lavy' brushed it off. Today Manning would have had to have a complete change of material, but he could tell a joke and could hold a note particularly a tenner!

Spike Milligan (1918-2002)

I never saw him perform live but was a fan from my teens. I read most of his war time books in the early 70's some of them at work when business was slack due to the three-day week. I started with "Adolf Hitler-my part in his downfall" and I was hooked.

In the 1950's he was the co-creator, main writer and performer (mainly as Eccles) in the Goon Show. It was before my time but I picked up some of its humour such as the character Bluebottle continually killed off; "you rotten swine, you deaded me". And little Jim's only line, in a childish voice "he's fallen in the water".

I did see his TV Q series which was to inspire some of the Monty Python team. Like Python its humour was patchy but could be hilarious. He got into trouble with his Curry and Chips show which would not be accepted today. Nor would his Pakistani Dalek from Q6.

I went to see a play called Ying Tong with Andy Bates in 2004. It was based on Milligan's battle with depression in 1960. Set in a psychiatric ward and radio theatre it amusingly featured some of the Goon Show characters in a very clever fashion.

His father was Irish, but he was born in India. Spike died aged 83 in 2002. He wanted "I told you I was ill" written on his gravestone. This was refused and a compromise was agreed with the phrase written in Irish.

Rob Brydon

I have always enjoyed watching Rob Brydon right from his early days when he created the character Keith Barrett who hosted a spoof TV chat show. He went on to successfully chair "Would I lie To You" and enjoy "The Trip" with Steve Coogan. He also starred as Uncle Bryn in the hugely successful "Gavin and Stacey".

Sue and I saw him perform his stand-up routine at the Royal Hall in Harrogate. He was very relaxed and of course amusing. He doesn't like being referred to as an impressionist, but he still gave us a bit of Michael Caine and his favourite,

Ronnie Corbett. We also heard from a "small man in a box".
All good stuff.

It took me some time to realise that three of the families in
Gavin and Stacey were named after British serial killers; West,
Shipman and Sutcliffe. Brydon played Bryn <u>West</u>. The two
lead characters were Gavin <u>Shipman</u> and Stacey <u>West</u>.
Gavin's parent's best friends were Pete and Dawn <u>Sutcliffe.</u> A
show well written and executed by Ruth Jones and James
Corden. He was at the same comprehensive school as Ruth
Jones in Porthcawl. His claim to fame is that he stole the lunch
money of fellow student Catherine Zeta-Jones at Dumbarton
House School.

12. SERIOUSLY GOOD TV

"The Soprano's, perhaps the greatest pop/culture masterpiece of its day"

Vanity Fair

I have enjoyed many tv series and I am therefore concentrating on those that have left a lasting impression.

Forsyte Saga 1967

Adapted from the John Galsworthy novel it told the story of the upper middle class Forsyte family. We watched the black and white production as a family every Sunday night at 7.25 from its launch on BBC1 in September 1968. It had been shown the year before on BBC2 to help promote the channel, which at the time had a potential audience of only 9 million. It would be some time before we replaced our old black and white model that had just the ITV and BBC1 channels.

We were hooked from the start. I had my 15th birthday the same month it started and quickly developed a teenage crush on Irene played by the actress Nyree Dawn Porter. At the same time, I developed a loathing of her brutal husband Soames, convincingly portrayed by Eric Porter. It was an excellent production due to a great cast which included Kenneth Moore as a Young Jolyon and the two weeks devoted to the rehearsal of each and every episode.

The series taught me two fundamental lessons: how gorgeous women could be and how they should be treated with respect, unlike the evil Soames. There were 26 episodes with the last shown in March 1969 and watched by 18 million viewers. Sadly, my dad wasn't one of them as he had tragically died of an unexpected heart attack the previous month.

It was not only a critical success in Britain and the USA as it became the first series to be sold to the Soviet Union.

The Prisoner 1968

A science fiction and psychological drama rolled into one "The Prisoner" was ahead of its time. It could not be more different than the Forsyte Saga, yet I watched the first episodes of both in the same month in 1968.

The plot centred on an unnamed British man (played by Patrick McGoohan the series co-creator) who resigns from his job, possibly as a spy for British intelligence. He is drugged and wakes up in a very strange coastal village.

McGoohan had previously starred as John Drake a spy in "Danger Man". My first thoughts were that he was playing the same character. However, the whole village set up was so intriguing you could read almost anything into it. If he tried to escape on the beach a giant balloon like ball known as "the Rover" would capture him and return him to the village. There were no names in the village just numbers. He was Number Six and spent half his time looking for Number One. "I am not a number I am a free man" was his cry, to no avail. He did keep a lid on the secrets his captors were seeking.

The ever-changing complex plots intrigued me. I stuck with it hoping for more clarity. Who was he? Where was he? Who were his captors? Would he ever escape? We never did get all the answers and that was half the glue that kept me there until the inconclusive ending.

"The Village" can be found in north Wales at Portmerion. It was designed and built by Sir Clough Williams-Ellis between 1925 and 1975. An Italian design said to be influenced by the Italian resort Portofino, the village has been visited by many well-known people including George Harrison who held his 50th birthday there. Today it is mainly a hotel and tourist attraction run by a charitable trust. I visited it in 1970 and was struck by the impression that the buildings were slightly smaller than they should be. It still had a lot of the magic of The Prisoner with Number Six's house clearly marked. I still have the entrance ticket showing 7/6d, a high price back then, but worth it.

Patrick McGoohan was of Irish descent although he was born in America in 1928 and died there in 2009. He was probably best known for his role as John Drake in "Danger Man" (retitled "Secret Agent" in America). The 4 series had 86 episodes with the length increased from 25 to 49 minutes after series 1.

He was a Catholic and is said to have turned down the role of James Bond in "Dr No" on religious grounds. He apparently did so again when considered for "Live and Let Die".

"Just one more thing". McGoohan wrote, produced, directed and appeared in several episodes of the American detective series Columbo. His actress daughter Catherine McGoohan appeared alongside him in his last episode; "Ashes to Ashes".

Survivors 1975-77

It is more than a little strange that I am writing this in the middle of a pandemic. Thankfully the current one at the time of writing is nowhere near as catastrophic as the one depicted in the 1975 TV series "Survivors". That "Survivors" pandemic was blamed on the accidental release of a virus by a Chinese scientist. Spooky or what? It was created by Terry Nation the man who gave us the Daleks and Blakes 7.

I can clearly remember the first episode where Abby (Carolyn Seymour) wakes up after the illness to find she is alone. Her husband has not survived, and her world has changed for ever. She sets off to try to find her son who is at boarding school many miles away. She soon meets up with the two other main characters Jenny (Lucy Fleming) and Greg (Ian McCulloch).

I was fascinated by how people would survive in a world where virtually everyone on the planet has died (Only one in

5000 surviving) and the modern world has completely shut down.

There were three series featuring 38 episodes. Terry Nation left at the end of the first series and budget cuts affected the third.

The BBC brought a new version to our screens in 2008. The main characters were retained with a stronger focus on action. It had mixed reviews but had strong audience figures. There were two series, but it failed to survive for a third.

Poldark 1975-77

The main reason for watching the Poldark series was due to the appearance of Kevin McNally as Poldark's brother-in-law Drake Carne. We were at Central Grammar School in the late 1960's and both played pirates in the school production of "Pirates of Penzance". As Poldark aired, Kevin was just starting to make a name for himself and had appeared in the popular tv series "I Claudius". He also had a small part in "Survivors".

He appeared in 13 episodes as Demelza's brother. Of course, the portrayal of his sister by Angharad Rees was another good reason for watching even if I could never pronounce her first name correctly. Comedian Eric Morecambe jokingly referred to her as "Hand Grenade Rees".

After a long pursuit Kevin's character Drake marries Morwenna (Jayne Wymark, daughter of actor Patrick Wymark the star of the 1960's "Power Game"). Kevin has had a very successful TV, radio, theatre and film career.

Moses the Lawgiver 1976

Although there were only six one-hour episodes of this series it had lots to offer. A strong cast led by Burt Lancaster as Moses and Anthony Quayle as his brother Joshua. It also had fantastic scenery having been filmed in Israel, Rome and Morocco.

I was working at the Leeds branch in Temple Row Birmingham when the series began. Every Monday morning my friend Andy would say "did you watch Moses?" and I would reply with just one word, "Rock". This went on for all six weeks.

Burt Lancaster's son Bill played the part of the young Moses just as Charlton Heston's son Fraser had played the young Moses in the 1956 film "The Ten Commandments".

Roots 1977

Based on Alex Hayley's book of the same name this unusual series fascinated me from the start. The story of Kunta Kinte being captured in the 1760's by slave traders in Africa and then treated appallingly as a slave in America is both thought provoking and heart-breaking.

It was a true mini-series as it had only 8 episodes but still managed to make a tremendous impact. When originally broadcasted in America it was shown on 8 consecutive nights. In the UK the BBC broadcast it in 6 parts. The first 3 on the weekend 8th to 11th April 1977 followed by the following 3 Sundays.

The viewing figures were incredible, particularly in America. It had 37 Emmy nominations winning 9 awards. It remains one of America's most watched programmes.

I was so moved I went straight out and bought the book. I still find it incredible that the African tribes could learn and then recite the lines of families going back many, many years.

Blake's 7 1978-81

Writer Terry Nation pops up again this time creating and writing the science fiction series "Blake's 7". It was a low budget series with some critics even comparing the wobbly sets with the production values of the Crossroads Motel. How dare they! Sue and I enjoyed all four series venturing across the universe aboard the spaceship Liberator. We enjoyed it so much we named one of our twin daughters Jenna after the character Jenna Stannis (Sally Kynvette). Or was it after Jenna Wade in Dallas? My favourite character was Vila the crafty thief who could pick any lock. He would have been perfect if he had another "L" in his name (up the Villa).

It ran for 4 series with 52 episodes from January 1978 to December 1981. It was popular with regular audiences of 10 million viewers. It ran its course and even the leader of the crew Blake himself only made guest appearances in the 3rd and 4th series.

Hill Street Blues 1981-87

Created by Steven Bochco (La law, NYPD Blue) this cop show was set in the police precinct of an unnamed American city. It was gritty but also had humour and poignancy. There was a mixture of long running story lines and also those wrapped up in one episode.

Lots of characters to love. Captain Frank Furillo (Daniel J Travanti) was a great role model for effective leadership and man management. Perhaps less so for domestic morality as he conducted an on-going affair with public defender Joyce Davenport (Veronica Hamel). I also loved the role of Mick Belker (Bruce Weitz) who ended up in all sorts of difficult situations due to his determination to get the case solved.

Sgt Esterhaus would end his daily briefing with "Let's be careful out there". When the actor Michael Conrad sadly died during series 4, Sgt Lucy Bates (Betty Thomas) said the same words until the end of the series.

It ran for 7 seasons with 146 episodes. It had 98 Emmy nominations winning 8 awards. Its production style included the use of handheld cameras that would influence many other shows. For me it was the best ever cop show. It also has a memorable theme tune written by Mike Post.

Not surprisingly our viewing habits changed when the children arrived in 1983 and 1984. More "Thomas the Tank Engine" and "Postman Pat" and more sleep when possible.

The Sopranos 1999-2007

Steve was born 1983 and Jenna and Claire followed in '84. For me there were no more memorable drama series until the Sopranos arrived in 1999. Steve and I watched it together and we loved it. Yes, it was violent at times, but it also had humour, action and even romance. The lead role of Tony Soprano (the late James Gandolfini) was cleverly pitched so viewers could love a hardened criminal. The only disappointment was the way the very last episode ended, dividing its loyal followers.

The West Wing 1999-2006

Created by the very talented writer Aaron Sorkin it started in the same year as the Sopranos and was a great political rollercoaster. It felt so real as even the most complex storyline made sense and was entirely believable. Giving President Bartlet (Martin Sheen) MS was a master stroke. Enjoyable from start to finish.

Band of Brothers 2001

Two years later I was enthralled by Band of Brothers the WW2 story of the American army's Easy Company fighting their way across Europe. It was produced by Steven Spielberg and Tom Hanks who had worked together on the hugely successful WW2 film Saving Private Ryan. The series gave me a new perspective on the role of America on the European side of the conflict. The lead character was Major Winters (Damian Lewis). This was a big break for Lewis who went on to play the lead role in the hugely successful "Homeland".

Six Feet Under 2001-05

Steve and I also enjoyed this series about the lives of a family funeral business. Particularly memorable was the final episode which shows a rapidly flowing montage of each of the characters' lives unfolding over the coming years. Two brothers ran the Fisher family funeral business after their father died. The introduction of the father as a ghost was very clever and fitted in with story line. The brothers, Nate and David were very different, and a younger sister Claire gave the family an interesting dimension.

It was a tremendous series for Michael C Hall (David) who went on to play the lead and title role in Dexter (2006-13)) which Sue and I both enjoyed despite the fact he killed someone every week.

The Wire 2002-2008

The Wire featured a different theme in each of the five seasons. It kept many of the characters throughout with English actor Domonic West benefiting from his lead role. Another cleverly written gritty series exposing many of the darker sides of a big American city. Based in a crime ridden Baltimore it would not have done much for tourism. Interestingly the city has successfully experimented with only chasing serious crime and not prosecuting small drug offenders or prostitutes. Crime has fallen considerably along with a substantial drop in reported violence and the policy is set to continue.

Spooks 2002-2011

This is the only British series that stands out in my memory. The 9-year run had 10 series. It did manage to make the British Secret Service look good most of the time. The plots were well written, and the influx of new characters was well balanced with the regulars. The actress Keeley Hawes (Missing, The Durrell's, Line of Duty) benefitted both as an actress and personally as she met and married co-star

Matthew Macfadyen. Another actress to benefit was Nicola Walker (Last Tango in Halifax, Unforgotten).

Breaking Bad 2008-13

An overqualified and underpaid chemistry teacher (Walter White, played by Bryan Cranston) is diagnosed with terminal lung cancer. He decides to find a way to make sure his wife and disabled son are financially secure. His plan is to use his chemistry knowledge to produce and sell the drug Crystal Meth.

The main character was portrayed cleverly to make viewers almost accept his methods. He brought in a former pupil Jesse (Aaron Paul) as his assistant and conduit to the criminal fraternity. There were 5 seasons and 62 episodes all set in New Mexico. It had everything a series needs, a great twisting plot, intrigue, humour and heart break. It won just about every TV award and in 2013 it entered the Guinness World Records as the most critically acclaimed show of all time.

Mad Men 2007-2015

Set in the world of advertising in the 1960's it was great entertainment. The main character Don Draper (Jon Hamm) was the womanising advertising executive with a hidden past. Another character Peggy Olson was played by Elisabeth Moss who has gone on to play a starring role in "Top of the Lake" and "The Handmaiden's Tale". It is now regarded as one of the greatest ever TV shows. I just about managed to see the last episode in 2015 before I lost the ability to follow any TV series.

Losing most of my vision and hearing now prevents me from watching anything other than a bit of sport. I can make out a dart board and snooker table. If I get close enough to the screen, I can just about follow a football and cricket with slow motion action replays. Sadly, no more on-screen drama for me.

13. STAND OUT FILMS FROM MY YOUTH

"Cinema should make you forget you are sitting in a theatre".
Roman Polanski

I have always loved going to the cinema. The last film I saw on the big screen was "12 years a slave". Not the best film I have seen but I miss going immensely.

Summer Holiday (1963)

This film starring Cliff Richard was released in January 1963 and my mom took Steve and I to see it during the school summer holidays at the Adelphi in Hay Mills. I was 9 years old and enjoyed it. It wasn't so much the music it was more the thought of turning a double decker bus into a travelling home that captivated me. Some 30 years later I would sit and have tea with Una Stubbs who played Sandy in the film.

It was a real feel good film with cheerful music helped by the talented Shadows, Cliff's real life backing group playing themselves.

Cliff turned 80 in November 2020 and is still going strong, releasing an album to commemorate becoming an octogenarian. He was set to appear on "Desert Island Discs" 60 years after his last appearance in 1960. This is the longest gap for a guest returning to the popular radio programme.

Summer Holiday was turned into a stage musical opening in Blackpool in 1996 with Darren Day taking Cliff's lead role as Don.

The Sting (1974)

The Sting's incredibly clever plot had me truly spellbound. The main stars Paul Newman and Robert Redford had achieved great success with their partnership in Butch Cassidy and the Sundance Kid a couple of years earlier. "The Sting" had the same director, George Roy Hill.

The film centres around a well worked and very complex "con". Set in the 1930's it leads to the eventual sting when the money is taken. The well worked and intricate operation was accompanied by appropriate music featuring Scott Joplin's "The Entertainer".

The film was incredibly successful winning 7 Oscars including best picture. It cost only $5 million to make but grossed over $150 million at the box office.

I was so taken with the film that I bought the book. I thought it would be the book that the film was based on. That was not the case as the book was pretty much the screenplay of the film. I still enjoyed it.

Easy Rider (1970)

There are several reasons why this film stands out for me. The first is that I saw it twice in 4 days both times with my girlfriend Elaine Jenkins at the Rock cinema in Saltley. The first visit was to see the film. The second visit was due to the youth club disco being cancelled at St Peters church Washwood Heath not far from the Rock.

The second memorable thing was we didn't watch much if any of the film on the second visit. I didn't think much of the film itself plot wise, but the music was, and is, pretty good. Born to be Wild is a classic with the Weight and The Pusher not far behind.

It was an independent production written by the lead actor Peter Fonda (Jane's brother and Henry's son) with co-star Dennis Hopper directing. It was a surprising success costing less than $500k to make and grossing $60 million. Many years later I bought the deluxe DVD and booklet and found myself actually finding the film more interesting probably due to fewer distractions!

The Graduate (1968)

This is memorable as it was the first X-rated film I saw. I went with my very good school friend Mark Ford. As we went into the Beaufort cinema, I stretched my body trying to look taller and older to get past the box office. We were admitted although I don't think I fooled anyone.

It was the first time I had seen Dustin Hoffman perform and he was pretty convincing as a 21yr old graduate having an affair with an older woman played by Anne Bancroft then falling in love with her daughter (Katherine Ross). In real life Hoffman (30) was only 6 years younger than Bancroft (36) who was positioned as his mother's age. Amazingly it worked. Doris Day turned down the Mrs Robinson role because of the nudity required. Natalie Wood turned down both the role of Mrs Robinson and her daughter Elaine.

The best thing about the film was the music written by Paul Simon and performed with Art Garfunkel. The four great tracks are Mrs Robinson, Sound of Silence, Scarborough Fair and the lovely April Come She Will. I bought the EP with all four tracks on and treasured it.

The film was a great success grossing over $100 million at the box office even though it only cost $3 million to produce. Director Mike Nichols won an Oscar and Hoffman and Bancroft were nominated for best actor and actress. The film was nominated for Best Film but was beaten by "In the heat of the night".

The Devils (1972)

I have included this Ken Russell film for the simple reason that it is the only film I have walked out on. I can't remember much about the film as we didn't stay long. I am no prude, but the violence and sadistic actions were just too much for us. The critics gave it a hard time and it was banned in many countries and edited for quite a few others. Amazingly it did well at the box office in the UK possibly attracting those who enjoy such outpourings. The lead roles were portrayed by the established actors Oliver Reed and Vanessa Redgrave. It was written by Ken Russell based on the book The Devils of Loudon by Aldous Huxley.

The Exorcist (1974)

I don't really go in for horror films mainly due to rarely being swallowed into the intended reality. But this one got me well and truly devoured. I went to view it with my late brother Steve and an open mind.

I was ok until the exorcism began and the young girl, Regan, spoke. Many people have been traumatised by the head turning right round. I had little trouble with that, but her voice went right through me sending shivers down my spine.

I was relieved once we set foot outside the cinema on the Bristol Road and headed for the pub. There was a group of people outside handing out leaflets and offering support for those suffering. I have still got the leaflet which gives phone numbers offering counselling. I did not suffer any adverse effects and slept well but would not bother to go to see any of the follow ups.

It made a lot of money as it only cost $12 million to make and grossed $440 million. I am sure that made a few heads turn!

The Towering Inferno (1975)

Some like it hot and this film certainly was. It had everything. A great storyline, plenty of pace and drama. Add to that a great cast and you have a winner.

The producer Irwin Allen had already produced an excellent disaster movie, "The Poseidon Adventure". Five of the less well-known actors from that film including Allen's wife appeared in this one. The two lead actors were Paul Newman and Steve McQueen. They both wanted to be seen as the lead role and eventually accepted a joint billing and a $1 million fee. Fred Astaire was in his 70's and put in a good performance as a con man earning him an Oscar nomination.

We were convinced that the cinema turned the heating up as the film progressed. Not all the people in the tower block survived but we were able to put our coats back on at the end as we left the heat of the cinema for a cold lager.

Summer of 42 (1971)

I was very fortunate to have John as a friend whose mother (Doreen Lavender) worked at ABC New Street and had a free pass for two people. John and I were regulars watching whatever was on, from lots of Hammer Horrors to Bonnie and Clyde or Bullitt.

In July 1972 John went on holiday with his parents and he very kindly let me have the free pass. I went with my good friend Gary Durant. We knew little if anything about the film but we both really enjoyed it. It was a low budget ($1 million) coming-of-age story that went much further.

A young wife (Jennifer O'Neill) widowed during the Second World War is befriended. She was vulnerable and eventually comforted (seduced would be too strong a word) by a young teenager on holiday. It is a one-way romance that is both very moving and at times amusing. It was very successful at the box office grossing more than thirty times the $1 million production costs.

It was very different from all the other films I had seen and would ever see. I found out afterwards that there was a book written before the film. When I bought the book, all was revealed. It was another Sting. Although published prior to the film it was based on the screenplay written for the up coming film. It was like watching it again, which was no bad thing.

The actress, model and writer Jennifer O'Neill is better known for marrying NINE times including twice to the same man. She also famously accidentally shot herself in the stomach and was fortunate to survive.

A Clockwork Orange (1973)

Directed and produced by Stanley Kubrick and based on the book by Anthony Burgess this is another very different film. It could be argued that this violent gang film was no better than The Devils. It was heavily criticised for its violent scenes and banned by many countries. Indeed, Kubrick withdrew the film from general release in Britain and many other countries.

The gang leader was played by Malcolm McDowell when he was in his late 20's. This is probably his most notable role but he has appeared in many other films, television shows and stage plays.

In my 1973 diary I rated it as "very good". Maybe the futuristic setting helped put the violence in a different place rather than a view of actual history. It was certainly an interesting and clever technical production by Kubrick that led to a number of awards. Maybe it is just the fact that I have always enjoyed an orange!

Don't Look Now (1974)

This is one of my very favourite films. Based on a short story by Daphne du Maurier and published in 1971. Brilliantly directed by Nicolas Roeg it grows and grows with hints of the supernatural to arrive at a tremendous climax.

The story focuses on the attempts of a married couple played by Donald Sutherland and Julie Christie to come to terms with the tragic loss of their young child. In addition to the gripping story is probably the best executed sex scene in the history of the British cinema. It was so beautifully put together that there have been countless claims that there was more than just good chemistry between the actors. Both have denied it, but speculation remains.

Much of the film is set in Venice giving it a marvellous background and adding to the suspense. The ending is both unexpected and shocking.

I continued visiting the cinema until my sight and hearing prevented me enjoying a good film.

If I had to pick out one film from 1974 to when I stopped it would be **Schindler's List (1993).** When John Lavender and I went to Poland in 2014 we visited the building where Oskar Schindler's factory was based in Krakow. I stood in his office and felt a real connection with this brave man who saved 1200 Jews from certain death.

"I think Schindler's List will wind up being so much more important than a movie. I don't want to burden it too much, but I think it will bring peace and goodwill to men".

Jeffrey Katzenberg chairman of Walt Disney Studios

14. SPORTING HIGHS

"Whoever said "it's not whether you win or lose that counts" probably lost".

Tennis legend Martina Navratilova

Football World Cup Toulouse 1998

Head of IS (information Systems) at the Halifax was Grahame Wright, a fellow Midlander and Villa supporter. He wandered into my office and casually said "fancy a free trip to a World Cup match in France?'. "What's the catch" I replied. "It is a 4-day trip with a supplier, and we will have to get permission from above". He didn't mean the Pope or Archbishop of Canterbury just the Personnel Director John Lee. The only way the supplier could get the tickets was by buying the extended four-day package.

We got official permission and were soon on our way to Toulouse. I couldn't wait as there was no time to lose (I know, I know). I had met our host Gerry on a previous "jolly" golf day at Brocket Hall. There were a couple of other guests, the CEO of the Coventry Building Society and Gary Hoffman head of Barclaycard.

We had a great time in the build-up to the group game against Romania. This included a game of golf at the impressive Toulouse Golf Club. I didn't play well and lost my usual number of balls. Our hotel was in the town square where we were regularly entertained watching almost constant games of football with about 30 England fans per side. Far less entertaining was the sight of an elderly lady using the pavement to relieve herself in broad daylight. I will spare you the details.

The actual match was a disappointment as we suffered a last-minute defeat to a goal scored by the Chelsea player Dan Petrescu. England's Michael Owen, aged 18, had brought the scores level in the 83rd minute but we left the ground a little downcast after the late strike. We managed to lift our spirits with an excellent last night meal. The French are well known for not over cooking their steaks and I ordered mine very well done which arrived with only small traces of blood and no movement.

Rugby League World Cup (1995)

The merger of the Leeds PBS and the Halifax took place in 1995. Shortly after the two came together I was invited to both the opening game of the Rugby League World Cup against Australia, and the final, both to be held at Wembley stadium.

Brought up in the West Midlands where rugby union was the only rugby game in town my exposure to the league version was limited to Eddie Waring's Saturday afternoon mud larks. I saw this as a good opportunity to meet new colleagues in a relaxed environment.

Australia were the favourites to win the tournament which comprised of 10 teams split into 3 groups (4,3,3). England were in the same group and managed to squeeze past the Aussies 20-16 in front of over 40,000 including me. My clearest memory of the day was watching the former T'Pau singer Carol Decker perform a song "one heart" specially written for opening the event. She had split up from T'Pau member Ron Rogers and was for a while a single Decker.

Both teams made it through to the final held just 3 weeks later. Australia returned to form winning 16-8. The bonus for me was being able to watch Diana Ross perform live before the kick-off.

Snooker World Championship 1984

I was the Leeds PBS manager in Hull from 1983 to '85 and on occasions frequented the George pub in the famous street, "the Land of Green Ginger". It was there that a trip to the snooker World Championships was planned by the regular crowd of professionals enjoying the usual Friday get together. Tickets were bought and a coach was booked to take us to the Crucible in Sheffield.

During the early stages of the competition the room is divided into two with a match in each section. We were fortunate to see Steve "interesting" Davis play and win his match. He had won the title the previous year and went on to win again beating Jimmy White 18-16 in the final.

I enjoyed the day. It was another tick in the sporting box, but I decided to give it a "rest". (this joke, right on cue)

FA Cup Final 2000

This was the first FA cup final I had been to. The last time the Villa had been in the final was in 1957 when thy beat Manchester United 2-1. This time Chelsea were our opponents. I was lucky to be sat high up on the gallery thanks to Halifax having a box there. The only slight downside was having to entertain a guest. Alex Brummer the financial editor of the Daily Mail was a pleasant enough chap, but he is a Chelsea fan. Like all fans I wanted to be able to shout and scream at my team not be having to behave at crucial moments. We lost 1-0 and didn't really deserve more than that. Alex was of course delighted. Poor me.

This was an historic match as it was the last FA Cup Final to be played before the twin towers were removed and the stadium revamped. Villa have been back, in 2015 getting thumped by Arsenal. My vision is now too poor for live football and I will unfortunately not be able to attend the new stadium.

League Cup Finals (6 times)

I have been to 6 of Villa's league cup finals. The first was against local rivals Birmingham City (1963). In those early days (this was only the tournament's third year) the final was played over two legs (home and away) before eventually moving to Wembley. We lost 3-1 on aggregate. The only thing

I can remember is being rescued by the police as I was about to disappear under the crowd trying to enter the ground with my brother Steve. Two memorable players were involved that day. The Blues captain was Trevor Smith who lived directly opposite us in Charminster Avenue, Yardley. The other was George Graham the Villa inside forward (midfield) who went on to play for Arsenal and Manchester United. Probably most remembered as a very successful manager at Arsenal before moving to manage both Leeds and Spurs.

I saw Villa Five times at Wembley; losing to Spurs in 1971, beating Norwich in 1975, Everton after two replays in 1977, Man Utd in 1994 and Leeds in 1996.

There were some stand out moments. Against Spurs I sat on a bench seat thanks to having one Villa share (cost £5) which gave me priority booking for a while. There were two replays against Everton. I went to the first at Sheffield Wednesday where I ended up standing on the roof of a refreshment kiosk, the only place I could find to watch the game. I couldn't make the winning game at Old Trafford but can remember screaming at the TV as centre half Chris Nichol scored from way outside the box to win the game.

My ticket for the Man Utd game was in the United section. Fortunately, a steward swapped me with a United fan stuck in the Villa section. It was not as good a seat as mine. It was just great to watch the boys win. The Leeds game was a virtual walk over as Leeds didn't turn up.

When the League Cup started in 1960 all 90 league clubs were invited. For the first few years as many as 10 declined. From the late 60's all 90 took part. Today many clubs treat it as an opportunity to involve more of their fringe players, especially those teams involved in Europe.

Open Golf (7 times)

I can thank a number of my work suppliers for an invitation to the Open Golf. They include IT specialists UNISYS who provided a computerised scoring system used by the BBC amongst others.

Four of my visits were in Scotland, St Andrews twice, Turnberry and Troon. In England I was lucky enough to go to Lytham St Annes, Birkdale and St Georges. All fantastic courses and usually great days out.

Memorable moments include driving up to St Andrews with my friend Dennis Skinner and being flashed by speed cameras at least 5 times but did not receive a single ticket. Probably ran out of film in those pre digital days.

In the late 1980's we were keen to sell pensions at the Leeds and I arranged for Prolific to make a presentation to the managers in the region. Afterwards the Prolific presenter asked me if I would like to be his guest at the 1988 Open Golf to be held at Lytham St Annes in July. On the Saturday of the tournament, he picked me up from home in Holmes Chapel under dark clouds. Before we got out of the village it was pouring with heavy rain. It didn't stop all day. The hospitality complex had to be closed as rain was coming through the roof and the weight of water was becoming a threat to bring everything down. The officials had no alternative other than to close the course after a short time and move everyone out. We only saw about an hour's play before we had to make our way out.

It was the first time the Open had played on a Monday to catch up. Seve Ballesteros was the eventual winner capturing his third Open Championship. The championship also broke the record for the lowest number of players (71) making the cut to play the final two rounds.

Ryder Cup Sept 2002

My Savings team at the Halifax had held a two-day savings convention at the De Vere Belfry hotel in Warwickshire. It was a big event attended by savings representatives from Halifax branches across the country. A few weeks later I received an invitation from the De Vere CEO to be his guest at the forthcoming Ryder Cup to be held in late September 2001 at the Belfry, also the home to the PGA (Professional Golf Association).

I received my instructions and was looking forward to attending and taking the opportunity to visit my mom who lived a relatively short drive away from the course. The 9/11 tragedy in America led to the event being postponed for a year. My loss of vision a few months later led to me ceasing work from the following February. De Vere very kindly confirmed that they would honour their invitation and I was delighted to take the train down to Birmingham and stay at my mom's.

As a VIP guest of De Vere I was in amongst the players and stood and watched them on the putting green. It was a great day. Superb hospitality and a great atmosphere watching a pretty even contest and keeping up to date by listening to the radio commentary. Europe had started the day one point ahead, but it was soon all square as we lost the opening match. It ended 8 points all by the end of the Saturday. I had enjoyed the day even with limited sight, watching the top players including Colin Montgomerie and Tiger Woods. Even so I thought it would be no hardship having to watch the final day on TV as it was hard to keep track of everything on the course even with my radio. The third and final day belonged to Europe, winning by 3 points.

The move to 2002 led to the decision to hold all the future fixtures on even years with the next one held in 2004 at Oakland Hills in the USA with Europe winning by a staggering 9 points. Due to the 2020 Covid pandemic the competition has again been put back a year to September 2021. This may lead to a return to holding the competition on years with odd numbers again.

Dubai, cricket, golf and F1

With our good friends Pam and Rick living out in the UAE I was very fortunate to be able make four visits which included some excellent sporting events.

During my first trip in 2009 I was able to watch through a telescope my adopted county Yorkshire play in a pre-season warm up competition at the Zayed Stadium. The stadium cost $23 million to build and opened in 2004.

My taxi driver was as clueless as I was when it came to finding the venue. After a few wrong turns we made it. I was one of about 30 spectators all sat in the main stand which had not been cleaned for a long while. I could get a cup of coffee, but the strange looking sandwiches held no attraction. Rick joined me later in the day for the closing overs. I was glad of the lift home particularly when I witnessed my one and only sandstorm. The main road became invisible until we got back into a built-up area where the buildings gave some protection.

The "Race to Dubai" is the climax of the European Golf Tour. The season's top 60 golfers compete for the annual title and substantial prize money. It is held at Jumeirah Golf Estate close to Dubai. Rick and I went to the very first tournament in 2009 won by Lee Westwood. We went again the following year to see Martin Kaymer win. The last time we went was in 2012 and were delighted to watch Rory McIlroy clinch the trophy. Over the four years the tournament grew with the addition of live bands, lots of food stalls and golf shops.

When Rick saw that the golf professional Robert Rock was taking part, we searched the course and found him on the 18th tee. He is quite easy to spot as he is the only professional I know that doesn't wear a cap. As he marched down the fairway with his caddie hauling his equipment, we moved alongside on the roped off path. Rick shouted over but Robert strode on. This was serious work for the golfer and didn't want to be distracted. Eventually he moved much closer, waved and said "Hi Rick". Apparently when Rock's wife had been a student, she lodged with Rick and Pam and they were invited to the Rock's wedding. Sadly, the Rock's weren't that solid and had split up.

The year we missed the golf was 2011. That year we decided to attend the F1 motor race held on Yas Island outside Abu Dhabi. It was the third time the F1 had been held on the manmade island. Pam and Rick's friend Jules came with us. We were all staying at Pam and Rick's lovely new apartment after their recent move from their old one.

I am not really into F1, probably more interested in what goes with it. There were lots of beer stalls and food concessions. The race itself was fairly uneventful apart from the fact that it started in the light at 5pm and ended in the dark. It was the only twilight Grand Prix of the season and a comfortable win for Lewis Hamilton.

After the race the fun started as we moved only a few yards to watch Paul McCartney perform with his band. I had seen him at the Sheffield Arena in 2003 with my good friend Andy Bates. Just as before he gave an excellent performance. The difference was the absence of his second wife Heather Mills dancing in front of the stage. The highlight was "Live and Let Die" where the whole arena lit up. Great end to an enjoyable day.

I am so grateful to Pam and Rick for their wonderful hospitality which we still enjoy now they live in nearby Harrogate.

For a full list of sporting events in the appendix at the end of the book.

15. SWINGING BUT DODGY

"The more I work and practice, the luckier I seem to get".

Golfer, Gary Player

As a child I enjoyed crazy golf and perhaps a bit of gentle putting at the seaside. My dad was a keen cricketer and tennis player. His good friend Peter Muddiman was a member at Hall Green golf club, but I don't think my dad ever strode the fairways of any course.

There are those who say that golf just spoils a good walk. I have found it offers a good deal more than that. For one thing it is probably the only sport where you can play at the same venues as the top professionals. Even as a very average player I have been lucky enough to play at many of the top courses including Wentworth and Loch Lomond. Loch Lomond is my favourite due to its excellent design, beautiful views and excellent condition.

Golf also has a scoring system that allows players of all abilities to compete. The handicap system is extremely fair and enables other formats to be effectively applied.

One in the eye

I think it was on the front at Eastbourne when I took my first full swing at about the age of 12. I had been watching the Open golf on tv and could not resist reproducing a swing that the great Jack Nicklaus may have approved of. The small putting area was however not really appropriate for such a demonstration. The first hole was only about 15 feet long, but I swung the putter high and made contact. Not with the golf ball. It was my dad that was clipped by my putter. He took it remarkably well and wore a plaster above his left eye for the rest of the week.

Pitch and putt

By the time I reached about 17 I graduated to the pitch and putt course at Tudor Grange Park Solihull. With friends and my brother Steve we had some great fun over the next couple of years. On one memorable visit Steve over hit his approach and hit a sign at the back of the green. His ball shot off and disappeared in the hole. The only problem was it was the wrong hole.

Proper golf

Despite us being beginners my friend John Watson was keen to play on a full sized 18 hole course. I took very little persuasion as I had just inherited a full set of clubs from Sue's Uncle Jim. We settled on Hatchford Brook municipal course on the Coventry Road. It was fine for those just starting to play except for the proximity of Birmingham airport running along one side. We played there three or four times before Sue and I moved to Somerset in 1979.

John was good company and we got on well. We also played football in the same league but for different teams. His wife Christine didn't like him playing football and resorted to occasionally hiding his boots. Not surprisingly John did not take kindly to this and not long after they unfortunately split up. Or was he "booted" out?

Back to basics

In June 1979 I was made manager of the Leeds Permanent Building Society in Bridgwater Somerset. In the October we were married and living in Cannington a very pleasant village about 3 miles from the branch. My new boss, Regional Manager Mike Rooke, was a nice chap, a bit old school but very supportive. He did have a bit of a hang up about me getting more involved in the local community. The Lions and Rotary clubs (too old), Round Table (too much boozing) were often mentioned. I was not interested despite the Leeds paying for everything. After about a year he turned to golf and

I became very interested. Membership was expensive at all the local courses but Mike told me it was not a problem as he would sanction it.

I investigated and it was an easy decision to book a lesson at Enmore Park golf club. Situated about 5 miles from Bridgwater it had a great reputation. I liked the professional's approach. He told me it was best to start from scratch as I would have picked up many bad habits. He soon proved that I had as he showed me how wrong my grip was. He lent me a 6 iron and gave me some routines to develop a correct swing. It had started well but before I could really progress I was moved back to the Midlands to open a new branch in Cannock. We were both delighted to be going close to home. I promised myself that one day I would return and actually complete 18 holes at Enmore. Sadly, this never happened.

The odd swing

Setting up a new branch in Cannock and a new home in Lichfield took up a lot of my time. Golf was pretty much put on the back burner. Uncle Jim's clubs did make a couple of appearances. My good friend Andy Bates was our manager of the Leeds branch in Lichfield. One of his agents was being passed over to the new Cannock branch so Andy arranged for us to meet up. Michael Bradford was an accountant based in Hednesford. Michael was a member at the Beau Desert golf club and suggested we meet up for a round at his club. Andy and I were both at the beginner's level, if that! Michael insisted and we gave it a go. We tried our best. I can remember making such a terrible shot at one hole that I literally collapsed in a heap of embarrassment which only made it worse. Down on your knees is simply not acceptable etiquette on a golf course. Michael took it all remarkably well and we made sure he had a great lunch when we finished.

My second outing whilst at Cannock was with another Leeds colleague Phil Whitehouse. We played it safe and went to a municipal course in West Bromwich. Phil was a good golfer and was just coaching me. Showing me how to hit certain kinds of shots. He was a good coach and I enjoyed it so much I stayed on my feet the whole time.

Our son Stephen was born on New Year's day 1983 at Good Hope hospital in Birmingham. On New Year's Eve I watched "A round with Allis". Peter Allis's guest was the Australian golfer Greg Norman. Allis's first words were "congratulations on the birth of your daughter Morgan". I burst out laughing. Morgan Norman. What sort of name is that? It made me think that if we had a son he would not be called Dan Duffin or a daughter Demi Duffin.

The lovely arrival of Stephen James Duffin meant that Jim's clubs went in the cupboard for quite a while. Cannock branch had been very successful and we were soon off to live in North Ferriby where I was set to manage our branch in Hull.

To Hull and back

Our Twin girls, Jenna and Claire arrived the next year which meant even more dust gathered on Jim's clubs until we moved two years later to Cheshire to manage the North Wales and Western region.

Our Crewe branch manager, Peter Maskrey, was a member of Crewe golf club not too far from our new home in Holmes Chapel. Peter invited me to play at his course. Afterwards he persuaded me to trade in Jim's clubs for a brand-new set. I didn't take much persuading as I was keen to blame the old clubs for my poor golf display.

The addition of a new set of clubs leaked out and I was invited to a few corporate golf days in the Warrington area where the regional office was based. My old friend Andy from Lichfield branch was now the manager of Warrington branch and we had a few fun rounds when invited by local business contacts.

We played at Walton Hill in a Pro-Am where a Professional joined each team of amateurs. Our host was the rally driver turned solicitor Roger Freeman one of Andy's business contacts. Andy and I played to our normal low standard and Roger and the pro weren't much better. At the first short par 3 hole somewhat amazingly the pro was the only one who failed to register a par.

Ducking and diving

In the summer of 1986, we arranged for about a dozen of the managers in the region to spend a couple of days at the beach resort of Rhosneigr on Anglesey. Despite the pouring rain a group ventured out on to the local golf course. This great weekend has now been repeated every year apart from the pandemic year of 2020.

The Rhosneigr course has at least two features I have not experienced anywhere else. Firstly, there are the sheep. I know there are a lot of the beasts in the green and pleasant Welsh countryside. You do not however expect to see them protecting a green or blocking a fairway. You do at the Rhosneigr golf course. About 99% of the time they move swiftly out of the way of an approaching ball. The numbers on the course have fluctuated over the years and are lower these days as the club tries to improve its reputation. One thing it can't do is prevent the RAF jets and helicopters screaming overhead as they take off and land from the adjacent runway. Or stifle the noise from the nearby railway line.

I have played in the annual event most years until my sight deteriorated to such an extent that even the sheep were difficult to spot. Each year the boys recall the occasion some years ago when I insisted on taking the very first stroke to open the round. One of the ground staff had parked his low trailer in front of the first tee. It didn't matter as the tee was elevated and it was therefore not blocking my drive as my ball would be way above the trailer's platform. I placed my tee and ball and confidently took a few paces back to line up. I addressed the ball and took a full swing. The ball was struck well but its trajectory was far too low. It struck the trailer and came back at me at full speed. I ducked as it flew over my shoulder and settled several feet behind the first tee. I was now about 15 yards further away from the hole than when I started. Not surprisingly the rest of the boys who had gathered at the side of the tee were in hysterics. Even I had to laugh. I knew then that this story would be retold and I have not been disappointed.

More golf and some improvement

In the middle of 1991. I was moved to our head office in Leeds. One of my colleagues, Stewart Taylor, was keen to play more golf and we joined a new club at Wike Ridge conveniently situated between my home in Wetherby and the centre of Leeds. This led to us sometimes playing 9 holes very early before work. We played there for 2 or 3 years as I waited for my name to move up the waiting list at Wetherby Golf Club. There were some stand out memories particularly the moment a hot air balloon came straight towards us descending rapidly. It landed right in front of us and managed to stay upright. As our nerves settled we played around it. A car appeared nearby which must have been following it and all was well.

I managed to win one competition and established a handicap of 23. My most memorable shot was a 7 iron from about 150 yds on the 17th hole which somehow ended up at the bottom of the awaiting cup.
In at last

I was eventually accepted as a member of my local club just over 5 minutes walk from our house. A lot of my friends played there and Sue and I enjoyed the social side of the club. Despite a number of lessons with the pro Mark my golf never really improved. This was mainly due to my pursuit of distance rather than accuracy.

After a couple of years one of our gang, I think it was Dennis Skinner, saw an advert in the Telegraph for a week's golf in Spain. It included 4 rounds of competitive golf, flights, accommodation and of course a copy of the Telegraph each day. In addition to Dennis we were joined by Ian Littlefair and Archie McDougall. We repeated our venture several times.

On our free days we often chose to play other courses rather than the two Mijas ones that were included. One year we were playing at Rio Real. We completed the front 9 without incident. When it was my time to drive at the 10th I hit a screamer. It was low, way to the right and heading for the halfway refreshment kiosk. Fortunately, it was closed with its metal shutter lowered. As my ball struck the shutter it made a huge sound. I made my way over and was pleased to find my ball as I was always low on "ammo". I also noticed that I was not the first offender as there were a number of ball sized dents in the screen.

We also played at Torrequebrada a challenging yet interesting course. To help my performance I had packed a small book of tips to help when you found yourself in a difficult position on a course. After a few holes my ball finished on quite a severe slope. Time to consult the tips book. I found the appropriate advice and lined up holding the club exactly as instructed. A good steady swing was followed by a smooth connection. My ball flew through the air and landed out of bounds. I could not believe it had sailed so far from my perfect line. Dennis came over and studied the book. "you adopted the perfect position for a downhill lie. Shame yours was uphill". We all burst into laughter as I threw the book back into my bag and searched for yet another ball.

Over several visits to Spain we managed quite a few prizes in the weekly competitions. I paired with Dennis and we won one of the competitions and were runners up on two other occasions.

We also visited Portugal one year with my next-door neighbour Chris Rollason joining the team. The weather was really bad when we played Salgados. The rain came down and the wind was blowing the ball at right angles. I gave up at the halfway mark and retreated to the club house for coffee. I had lost so many golf balls and I was really not happy. We played the very same course a few days later in perfect conditions and it was a real joy. What a difference a couple of days can make.

Emerging from the merger

The Leeds PB Society was swallowed by the Halifax in 1995. The following year we sent out a huge mailing with my name on the bottom. A phone call followed from a friend I hadn't seen since we had left Birmingham in 1979. Martin Wood and I arranged to meet up at the office of another missing friend Steve Clayton at his office in London. We went to a local pub and didn't stop talking and drinking. Eventually I stood in a huge taxi queue outside Liverpool street station. It became clear there was a major problem with the tube system causing the longest queue I had ever seen. I was standing there full of beer when a dazzling bright light lit up around me a huge microphone was stuck in my face. I was live on air and being questioned about the problem. I have no idea what I said but was told the next day that I did OK. It was local London news but I was still spotted.

The three of us arranged to meet up in Birmingham to play golf at Copt Heath near Knowle. A venture that was repeated for the next 25 years. Another friend from our youth, Rob Sherratt, has joined us for the last dozen years or so. We played for an old Grenville cricket bat we used to play with as kids. I never won it but I did hole out with a four iron from 170 yards on the 16th. There was a member of the ground staff by the hole who helpfully pointed to the hole when we were searching for my ball.

A bit embarrassing

In the early Halifax days the Bank of Scotland were processing our credit cards. As a gesture of goodwill they invited myself and my boss Judy Atchison to a round of golf and lunch at Bruntsfield Links in Edinburgh. It is one of the oldest golf courses in the world. Unfortunately at the time it had rules and regulations to match.

Lady members were not allowed and as we approached the first tee it was clear there were no ladies tees. The BOS guys were very apologetic and Judy just took it in her stride. A compromise was agreed and a good contest was enjoyed. As I sat down to lunch on a very hot day, I slipped off my jacket as I sat down. Before it settled on my chair a hand was on my shoulder as a waiter explained that jackets must be worn at all times unless the club captain gave permission, and he was not there.

I was invited again by BOS to the impressive Loch Lomond and Sunningdale courses. Jolly good jollies.

I do miss not being able to play the game or sample the social life due to my severely impaired sight and hearing but have many great memories to reflect on.

A full list of courses played can be found in the end of the book.

Appendices

- Bands/Acts Seen

- Musicals

- Major sporting events

- Golf courses played

Bands/Acts Seen

Band/Act	Venue	Date	With
Gentle Giant	Mothers Erdington	10/07/1970	Mark Ford
Brett Marvin & the Thunderbolts	Mothers Erdington	19/07/1970	Brian Harris
Derek and the Dominoes (Eric Clapton)	Mothers Erdington	09/08/1970	Brian?
Edgar Broughton Band	?	21/09/1970	?
Procol Harum	B'ham Town Hall	25/09/1970	?
Jethro Tull	B'ham Town Hall	25/09/1970	?
Tir Na Nog	B'ham Town Hall	25/09/1970	?
Taste	B'ham Town Hall	30/09/1970	Bill (Co-op),John
Jake Holmes	B'ham Town Hall	30/09/1970	Bill (Co-op),John
Stone the crows	B'ham Town Hall	30/09/1970	Bill (Co-op),John
Free	B'ham Town Hall	06/10/.70	Mark, Sweat, John
Mott the Hoople	B'ham Town Hall	06/10/.70	Mark, Sweat, John
Pegasus	Central School dance	20/10/1970	Elaine
Demon Fuzz	B'ham Town Hall	11/11/1970	Elaine,John,Mark,Bri,Paul W
Comus	B'ham Town Hall	11/11/1970	Elaine,John,Mark,Bri,Paul W
Titus Groan	B'ham Town Hall	11/11/1970	Elaine,John,Mark,Bri,Paul W
Idle Race	Solihull Ice Rink	31/01/1971	Mark,Gaz,John
Raymond Froggat	Solihull Ice Rink	31/01/1971	Mark,Gaz,John
Agapus	Swan Pub	01/02/1971	Mark,Gaz,John+ lots of others
Bastille	Swan Pub	08/02/1971	Mark,Gaz,John+ lots of others
Deep Purple	B'ham Town Hall	12/02/1971	Bri,Gaz,John,Paul W,John Clegg
Hardin-York	B'ham Town Hall	12/02/1971	Bri,Gaz,John,Paul W,John Clegg
Free	B'ham Town Hall	24/02/1971	Elaine, Mark
Amazing Blondel	B'ham Town Hall	24/02/1971	Elaine, Mark
Heavy Boots	Harlequin	12/03/1971	John,Gaz,Sweat,Colin Bowater
Ghost	Harlequin	12/03/1971	John,Gaz,Sweat,Colin Bowater
?	Mayfair Suite	15/03/1971	John,Ste,David & Liz?
NationL GRID	Club?	17/03/1971	John,Gaz,Sweat, others
Ghost	Club?	17/03/1971	John,Gaz,Sweat, others
The Who	Mayfair Suite (Kinetic Circus)	12/05/1971	Bri,Gaz,Paul W
Stack Waddy	Bulls Head Cov' Rd	05/06/1971	John,Gaz,Bri,Paul W
Children	Hideaway	12/06/1971	John,Gaz,Bri,Paul W,JC
Galliard	Hideaway	16/06/1971	Mark,Gaz
Canyon	Hideaway	14/08/1971	Elaine,Yvonne,Gaz,Paul W
Canyon	Hideaway	04/09/1971	Elaine,Yvonne,Gaz,Paul W,John

Band/Act	Venue	Date	With
Ten Years After	B'ham Town Hall	04/10/1971	John,Gaz,Bri,Paul W
Keith Christmas	B'ham Town Hall	04/10/1971	John,Gaz,Bri,Paul W
Supertramp	B'ham Town Hall	04/10/1971	John,Gaz,BriPaul W
King Crimson	B'ham Town Hall	13/10/1971	John,Gaz,Bri,Paul W,Mark,Val
Flying Hat Band	Hideaway	16/10/1971	John,Gaz,Bri,Paul W,Tony S, Mick S
Mott The Hoople	B'ham Town Hall	01/11/1971	John Clegg
Peace	B'ham Town Hall	01/11/1971	John Clegg
Uriah Heap	Mayfair Suite (Kinetic Circus	11/11/1971	Mick S,Gaz,Bri
Anibus	Kinetic Circus	11/11/1971	Mick S,Gaz,Bri
Family	B'ham Town Hall	12.11/1971	Mick S,John,Paul W
America	B'ham Town Hall	12.11/1971	Mick S,John,Paul W
Money Jungle	Hideaway	13/11/1971	?
Led Zeppelin	Kinetic Circus	17/11/1971	Mick S,Gaz,Bri
Emerson Lake and Palmer	Oden New St B'ham	11/12/1971	Gaz
Michael Chapman	Oden New St B'ham	11/12/1971	Gaz
Anibus	Central School dance	15/12/1971	Elaine,Fiona,Yvonne
Curved Air	B'ham Town Hall	17/12/1971	John,Gaz,Bri,Paul W,Girls
Skid Row	B'ham Town Hall	17/12/1971	John,Gaz,Bri,Paul W,Girls
Procol Harum	B'ham Town Hall	19/01/1972	Elaine,Fiona,Yvonne,G,J,PW,JC
Amazing Blondel	B'ham Town Hall	19/01/1972	Elaine,Fiona,Yvonne,G,J,Sh,JC
Wishbone Ash	B'ham Town Hall	28/01/1972	John C
Free	B'ham Town Hall	02/02/1972	Elaine,Yvonne,Gaz,Bri,John
Sutherland Brothers	B'ham Town Hall	02/02/1972	Elaine,Yvonne,Gaz,Bri,John
Mountain (Les West)	Kinetic Circus	07/02/1972	Elaine,Yvonne,Gaz,Paul W,Bri
Strawbs	B'ham Town Hall	15/02/1972	Elaine,Fiona,Yvonne,Gaz,Bri
Osibisa	Kinetic Circus	16/03/1972	Bri
David Bowie	B'ham Town Hall	17/03/1972	Bri,Gaz
Mr Crisp	B'ham Town Hall	17/03/1972	Bri,Gaz
Mungo Jerry	Top Rank	28/07/1972	Pete Olive
Faces	Kinetic Circus	22/10/1972	Pete Olive,John,JC,Ste C
Emerson Lake and Palmer	Oden New St B'ham	24/11/1972	?
Barclay James Harvest	Wolverhampton Civic Hall	27/11/1972	Bri,Ste,Keith
Camel	Wolverhampton Civic Hall	27/11/1972	Bri,Ste,Keith
Family	B'ham Town Hall	06/12/1972	JC,Pete,Bri,John,Keith
Dire Straits	NEC B'ham	?	Sue,Paul,Wendy Thomson.
M People	Manchester Arena	1991?	Sue,Pam,Rick
Genesis	Rhoundhey `park Leeds	1993?	Sue, Ed,JaneTemps
Jimmy Nail	Sheffield Arena	1995?	Sue + locals
Elton John	Wembley Stadium	1997?	Sue BOS couple
Shirley Bassey	Sheffield Arena	1999?	Sue +BT

Band/Act	Venue	Date	With
Fleetwood Mac	NEC Arena	25/11/2003	Martin Wood
Fleetwood Mac	Sheffield Arena	02/11/2009	Andy Bates
Paul McCartney	Sheffield Arena	06/04/2003	Andy Bates
Paul McCartney	Abu Dhabi	Nov-11	Pam, Rick and friends
Queen and Paul Rodgers	B'ham Symphony Hall	Oct 2007	Martin Wood
Diana Ross	Wembley Stadium	7th Oc1995	Rugby Lge opening ceremony
Carol Decker	Wembley Stadium	28th Oct 95	Rugby Lge world cup final
Four Tops	Odeon Bham	13/11/1975	Frankie Smith
Susan Maughan	Butlins Minehead	1989	Firths
Paper Lace	Lyme Bay Hol Camp	1990	Firths
Paul Carrick	Royal Hall	18/11/2013	Firths
Tom Paxton& Janis Ian	Opera House York	28/03/2014	Stuart and Neil Rhodes
The Beach Boys	York races	25/07/2014	Pam,Rick Dennis,Barbara
The Real Thing	Warrington	Dec-91	Leeds Perm Staff

Musicals

Aspects of love (Prince of Wales 15/12/89 M Ball
Aspects of Love (Leeds)
Phantom of the opera (Her Majesty's) D Willetts
Phantom of the opera (Bradford Alhambra))
Sunset Boulevard (Adelphi)
Whistle down the wind
Joseph (Leeds)
Bombay dreams
Miss Saigon
Martin Guerre (West Y P 30/11/98)
Lion King
Mamma Miia
Buddy (Leeds)
Blood Brothers (Phoenix) Stephanie Lawrence
Blood Brothers (Leeds) Bernie Nolan
Priscilla Queen of the desert
Top Hat
Saturday Night fever
Grease (Bradford Alhambra)
Jesus Christ SS (Grand Leeds) 28/11/98
Chicago (London)
Motown, Royal Hall Harrogate 16/5/2014
West Side Story, Leeds Grand 23/5/14
Dirty dancing (London)
Singing in the rain (West Y P Leeds)
Little shop of horrors (West Y P)
Spamalot (Leeds)
Hair (B'ham)
Rocky Horror Show (Bradford Alhambra)
Jersey Boys (London)
Les Miserables (Bradford Alhambra) 25/6/98
We Will Rock You (London)
Gypsy (Leeds)
Annie (Leeds)
Oliver (Leeds)
The Pirates of Penzance (Leeds) Paul Nicholas '97
Carmen (Leeds)1999
South Pacific (Leeds)
Billy Elliot
Smokey Joe's Caffe (New York) Dec 97
Acorn Antiques
Five guys named MO (West Y P)
Half a Sixpence (West Y P) 29/12/200
Barber of Saville (Grand Leeds) 1998
Wicked Leeds Grand 13/6/2014
The Commitments London 2014
Thriller London 2015

Major Sporting Events

Soccer

Date	Event	Venue	Result
23rd May1963	League Cup final 1st leg	St Andrews	Blues 3 Villa 1
23rd Dec 1970	League Cup Semi 2d lg	Villa park	Villa 2 Man Utd 1
27th April 1968	FA Cup Semi final	Villa park	Bham 0 WBA 2
22nd Mrch 1969	FA Cup Semi final	Villa park	ManCity 1 Everton 0
27th Feb 1971	League cup final	Wembley	Villa 0 Spurs 2
1st March 1975	League cup final	Wembley	Villa 1 Norwich 0
12th March 1977	League cup final	Wembley	Villa 0 Everton 0
16th March 1977	League cup final reply	Hillsborough	Villa 1 Everton 0
27th March 1994	League cup final	Wembley	Villa 3 Man Utd 1
8th June 1995	Umbro cup	Elland Rd	Eng 3 Sweden 3 (last 2 mins)
7th April 1982	Semi-final Euro cup	Villa Park	Villa 1 Anderlecht 0
24th March 1996	League cup final	Wembley	Villa 3 Leeds 0
22nd June 1998	World Cup	Toulouse France	Romania 2 Eng 1
17th November 1999	Euro 2000 play off	Wembley	Eng 0 Scotland 1
2nd April 2000	F A Cup semi final	Wembley	Villa win on pens

Golf

Date	Event	Venue	Winner
14th July 1988	Open Golf	Royal Lytham	S Ballesteros
14th July 1994	Open Golf	Turnberry	N Price
20th July 1995	Open Golf	St Andrews	J Daly
17th July 1997	Open Golf	Royal Troon	J Leonard
16th July 1998	Open Golf	Royal Birkdale	M O'Meara
20th July 2000	Open Golf	St Andrews	T Woods
28th September 2002	Ryder Cup	The Belfry	Europe 15.5 to 12.5
18th July 2003	Open Golf	Royal St George Sandwich	Ben Curtis
19th November 2009	Race for Dubai	Jumeirah Golf Estates	Lee Westwood
27th November 2010	Race for Dubai	Jumeirah Golf Estates	Martin Kaymer
10th June 2011	PGA Seniors	Slayley Hall	Andrew Oldcorn
22nd Nov 2012	Race for Dubai	Jumeirah Golf Estates	Rory McIlroy

Rugby Union

Date	Event	Venue	Winner
19th February 1994	International	Twickenham	Eng 12 Ireland 13
18th March 1995	International	Twickenham	Eng 24 Scotl'd 12
1st March 1997	International	Twickenham	Eng 20 France 23
15th March 1997	International	National Stadium Cardiff	Eng 34 Wales 13

Rugby League

Date	Event	Venue	Winner
7th Oct 1995	World cup kick off	Wembley	Eng 20 v Aust 16 Diana Ross
28th Oct 1995	World cup final	Wembley	Eng 8 v Aust 16 Carol Decker

Cricket

Date	Event	Venue	Winner
19th June 1980	2nd Test	Lords	Drawn Gooch 123
25th May 1989	1st ODI	Old Trafford	Eng win by 95
27th July 1989	4th test	Old Trafford	Aus win by 9 wkts
7th August 1992	5th test	Oval	Pak win by 10 wkts
19th July 1993	Durham v Australia	Durham University raceco'	Ian Botham retires drawn
14th July 1994	Durham v S Africa	Chester-le street	drawn
1st Sept 2001	C&G Final	Lords	Som win B0 9 wides in 2 overs
5th 6th Jan 2003	5th Test	Sydney Cricket Ground	Eng win by 225
1st 2nd 3rd April 2004	3rd test	Ken' Oval Barbados	Eng win by 8wkts
0th to 14th April 2004	4th test	Recreation Grd Antigua	Drawn Lara 400
3rd to 7th June 2004	2nd Test	Headingley	Eng win by 9wkts
2nd to 6th JAN2005	3rd test	Newlands	S Afica win byY 196 Kallis 149
18th-22nd March 2006	3rd test	Wankhede Mumbai India	Eng win by 212
4th-6th Aug 2006	3rd test	Headingley	Eng win by 167 runs v Pakistan
23rd to 27th Nov 2006	1st test	GABA Brisbane	Aus win by 277
1st to 5th Dec 2006	2nd Test	Adelaide Oval	Aus win by 6 wkts
25th -7th May 2007	2nd test	Headingley	Eng win by inngs
d Sept 2007	5th Odi	Headingley	India in by 38 runs
5th-9th March 2008	1st test	Hamilton	New Z in by 189 runs Taylor 120
13th-17th March 2008	2nd Test	Wellington	Eng win by 126 runs Ambrose 102
19th/20th July 2008	2nd test	Headingley	S Africa win by 10wkts
22nd Aug 2008	1st Odi	Headingley	Eng bt SA by 20

Date	Event	Venue	Winner
4th-7th Feb 2009	1st Test	Sabina Park Jamaica	WI win by inngs
30th/31st July 2009	3rd Test	Edgbaston	Drawn
7th -9th Aug 2009	4th Test	Headingley	Aust win by ing+ 80 runs
3rd-7th Jan 2010	3rd test	Newlands SA Cape Town	Drawn v SA
14th-18th Jan 2010	4th test	Wanderers SA j"burg	Eng lose to SAby igs
12th Sept 20110	2nd Odi	Headingley	Eng win by 4wkts
1st July 2011	2nd Odi	Headingley	Sri L win by 69 runs
6th July 2011	4th Odi	Trent Bridge	Eng win by 10 Wkts
30th July 2011	5th Test	Trent Bridge	Eng win by 319
3rd Sept 2011	1st Odi	Durham	no result India rain
26th -30th March 2012	1st test	Galle Sri Lanka	SL win by 75 runs
3rd-7th April 2012	2nd test	Colombo Sri Lanka	Eng win by 8wkts
2nd-5th Aug 2012	2nd Test	Headingley	Drawn V S A KP 149
24th -26th May 2013	2nd Test	Headingley	Eng beat New Z
1st-3rd Aug 2013	3rd test	Old Trafford	Drawn v Australia
20th-22nd june 2014	2nd test	Headingley	lost on last but one ball v Sri Lanka Broad Hat trick

Horse Racing

Date	Event	Venue	Winner
April 1988	Grand National	Aintree	
7th April 1990	Grand National	Aintree	Mr Frisk
19th August 1993	Ebor	York	
15th June 1993	Royal Ascot	Ascot	
20th March 19190	Cheltenham festival	Cheltenham	

Tennis

Date	Event	Venue	Winner
1st July 2013	Open	Wimbledon	Mens doubles semi finals Bryan Bros win

Snooker

Date	Event	Venue	Winner
Apr-84	Embassy World Chmp	Sheffield Crucible	Steve Davis

Table Tennis

Date	Event	Venue	Winner
Nov-88	International	Wrexham	Wales v Spain

Formula 1

Date	Event	Venue	Winner
13th November 2011	F1 world championship	Yas Marina Abu Dhabi	Lewis Hamilton

Miscellaneous

Date	Event	Venue
1989	Question of sport	Manchester
17th Jan 2014	Boycott and Aggers	Royal Hall Harrogate
13th Feb 2014	Blofeld and Baxter	Harrogate Theatre
3rd July 2014	Henley Regatta	Henley

Golf Courses Played

UK	UK/IOM	UK	Abroad
Wetherby	Belfry Brabazon	Loch Lomond	Mijas (Largos)
Moortown	Sunningdale	South Staffs	Mijas (Olivos)
Alwoodley	Bloxwich	Dalfaber	Rio Real
Copt Heath	Bridlington	Cookridge	Almenara
Rhosneigr	Scarcroft	Carden Park	La Cala
Headingley	Otley	Mere	Santa Maria
Pannal	Edgbaston	Woburn	Torrequbrada
York Strensall	Stratford Oaks		Los Narnjos Marbella
Turnberry	Sand Moor		Santana
Bruntsfield Links	Druids Heath		El Paraiso Estepona
Horsforth	Deane		Vilamoura 1
Wentworth (East course)	Lancaster		San Lorenzo
Malton and Norton	Ladbrook Park		Quinta do Gramacho
Ilkley	Slaley Hall		Vale de Pinta
Howley Hall	Sutton Coldfield		The Links (Florida)
Rudding Park	Menzies Welcome		The Dunes (Florida
Little Aston	King Edward Bay IOM		Toulouse (France)
Brocket Hall	Davenport		
Blackwell	Leeds		
Shrigley Hall	Hull		
Robin Hood	Castletown IOM		